It Started With A Kiss

Stanley Sipka

BALBOA.PRESS
A DIVISION OF HAY HOUSE

Balboa Press books may be ordered through booksellers or by contacting:

Balboa Press
A Division of Hay House
1663 Liberty Drive
Bloomington, IN 47403
www.balboapress.com
844-682-1282

Print information available on the last page.

ISBN: 978-1-9822-7762-8 (sc)
ISBN: 978-1-9822-7763-5 (e)

Library of Congress Control Number: 2021923390

Balboa Press rev. date: 04/16/2024

Contents

Epigraph

<u>"I have been the Nurse I always wanted to be, after all. I guess
I don't need a diploma on the wall to prove that"</u>

Words Joanne said to Cathy when she was in the Hospice facility hours before she died

<u>"Mrs. Sipka, can you help me?"</u>

This was the sentence that was heard constantly by Becky Devereaux and Jeanann Aikens as Joanne did her job helping the special education students at Roberts Middle School.

<u>I hope you haven't changed your mind about me!</u>

This sentence was in letters I received during my two years in the Army. I would hurry, write a letter, and send it so Joanne wouldn't wonder how I felt. Those words made me feel good to know I had a woman who wanted me. I wrote almost daily and ensured Joanne I didn't change my mind about her.

<u>Stan, don't worry, together we'll make it work!</u>

These types of words were typical of Joanne as we met daily challenges. She made me think I was the boss, and it worked. We were typical newlyweds wondering how we would live our lives and how long we would be together. Children? Grandchildren? Where would we live? What type of job would I have? Would Joanne have to work? These are just a few questions we answered over the 61 years. We were so engrossed in our duties as parents and spouses that the days turned into weeks, months, and years. Occasionally, we would sit, look back, and go ahead. She would ask me if I was her little boy. I would show her how much I loved her by extending my arms to the left and right and saying, this is how much I love you. I told her early in our marriage that she was like that catcher I had, who made me a successful pitcher because he knew how to call pitches. He knew my strengths and weaknesses and didn't care if I got all the credit. There were changes in our plans regarding our daughters and parents. We begin to experience those medical conditions like – glasses, heart attacks, hip operations, cataracts, gallbladder operations, muscle loss, hearing aids, and weight gains. She, standing behind me, nodding "no," convinces the Doctor to send me to the hospital just to check out this little pain in my neck that I thought was nothing. The next day, I had a stent placed in my heart.

Preface

This book is necessary to tell the world what an outstanding person Joanne Christine (Braghieri) Sipka was during the 83 years she lived. She was my loving wife and partner from the first day of our marriage, June 28, 1958, to October 11, 2019. Our blind date, with my quick kiss at the end of the date, led to 2 years of dating and 61 years of marriage. I, like most men, felt I would die first and worked to make Joanne's existence financially sound. We moved in with Joanne's mom in 2002 because Joanne worried about her mom at age 91. After Joanne's mom died in 2015, we became a couple again. Our advanced age limited our activities, and different medical problems arrived: hip and knee problems and the need for canes and walkers. Joanne worried about her blood counts and her medicines and was anxious and concerned about her diabetic condition. Jo didn't take insulin but was afraid of diabetes. She visited medical personnel who prescribed medicine that controlled her life. There was a constant battle to arrive at the correct dose of the mind-altering medication. There was a chart of when and what pills to take daily. She took her blood every morning and worried when her number was over an acceptable number. There were times when I would prick the finger, tip the little blade into the blood, and tell her the number. I would say it's "under" or "over." I would say it's OK a couple of times when it was just over the number.

Joanne's passing is hard to imagine. At a couple of bereavement sessions for men, I heard stories, looked at the men, and saw me in their grief. One man mentioned he could not enter their bedroom; he slept on the floor next to the couch she slept on for many months, sick with cancer unable to go upstairs to their bedroom. I could stay in our bedroom after telling myself that's what Joanne wanted me to do. I had to keep the family together to get through this upsetting event. What would I ask Joanne to do if I had died? For me, October 11 will be a quiet day with a visit to the cemetery. November 2, her birthday could be different this year. The family might plan something, and that's fine with me.

Returning from visiting a funeral home to pay respects for one of our friends' showing, we talked about what would each of us do if the other died. We joked about, "Would you let your new husband use my golf clubs?" her answer would be, "No, he's left-handed!" or would you let your new wife use my Ipad? "No, she has her own!"

My world is turned upside down, and I must continue for my family's sake. I feel responsible for them. Please help me, Joanne!

Acknowledgments

To my family and friends for their encouragement to continue this project.

My daughters and grandchildren and Joanne's Sister, Diane, helped by writing, reading, and making suggestions, adding their Tributes to Joanne – Mother and Grandmother.

A special thanks to Julia Sincel, my granddaughter, who helped combine the text with the documents.

A special thanks to Mrs. Sue Wells, neighbor, for her advice, suggestions, and article

To the Roberts Middle School staff and students for acknowledging Joanne's work as an aid in their program.

To Joanne's friends, Phyllis Falkenstein and Marilyn Barber

Prologue

TRIBUTE TO JOANNE

<u>Joanne C. Sipka, My Wife of 61 Years</u>

Everything I have is the result of meeting Joanne on a blind date in the spring of 1955. My first thrill was seeing her as she opened the door to greet me and Steve, who arranged the date. Silently, I said, "Wow! She's pretty!". We played miniature golf and did not care what our scores were. As the night ended, I walked her into her house, leaned over, and kissed her. I backed away, looked at her, and she said, "I don't let guys kiss me on the first date." I replied," there's always a first time for everything!". That was not the last kiss.

She attended Akron University and then worked for a doctor. We talked about marriage, but I had a six-year military obligation. I volunteered for the draft because we didn't want to be married and separated. We married on a beautiful, sunshiny day on June 28, 1958. I completed my Army responsibility, and we lived with her parents. She encouraged me to obtain more education, even though I attended Hower Vocational High School and lacked confidence in my academic background. She worked long hours while I attended Kent State University, and I worked part-time. In 1961, Joanne gave birth to Christine, Cathleen in 1963, and Carol in 1965. She had difficult and painful pregnancies, but after, she enjoyed happiness with her three beautiful daughters.

She enjoyed watching her daughters and grandchildren in sporting events and school activities, and in later years, encouraged me to return to playing baseball with the old "bad news bears,"

Her most rewarding accomplishment was she and I moved in with her mother after her dad died. Joanne mothered her mother and allowed her mother to enjoy life to the age of 103.

Joanne was always concerned about me, the three daughters, eight grandkids, and everyone else. All of us are who we are because of her.

Thank You, Joanne; I want to see you again and give you a kiss like the first one.

THERE SHOULD BE 2 PARTS TO THIS STORY. THE MAIN PART IS ABOUT JOANNE AND WHAT A GREAT PERSON SHE WAS TO ME, OUR DAUGHTERS, GRANDKIDS, FAMILY, FRIENDS, AND EVERYONE ELSE.

THE SECOND PART IS A WARNING ABOUT THE DEPRESSION, PANIC ATTACKS, AND THE MEDICINES PEOPLE TAKE TO OVERCOME WHAT JOANNE HAD. IT'S LIKE A WARNING TO OTHERS TO TAKE THOSE FAMILY MEMBERS' CONDITIONS SERIOUSLY AND WORK ON CORRECTING THOSE CONDITIONS. DON'T WAIT UNTIL IT'S TOO LATE. IT IS NOT EASY.

Introduction

Christine, Cathleen, Carol, and I walk down the hallway and enter a room with a single bed. There are few items of furniture. The one recliner chair was used by Cathy, who stayed all night. We walk to the bed and see Joanne breathing without devices assisting her. We greet her, kiss her, express our love, and each offers one hand to hold her hand. The five of us held hands and recited the Our Father together for the last time. I don't remember if anything was said; I was quiet. We wanted to take her home even now; I thought she would awake and return home. Her breathing was exciting to me. There was that normal rhythm, but it paused, and we all stared at her. The breathing continued, and we relaxed but stopped again. I kept saying silently, "keep going!" but it ended. We all cried and wanted her back; I wanted to go with her but couldn't. I went to a chair, sat, and thought this was a bad dream, and I would awake and see her next to me in bed. It was not a bad dream. That was October 11, 2019, at 1:30 in the afternoon. Joanne died.

<u>What Now?</u>

Joanne was in the hospital and other facilities for 88 days. I thought she would return home for the first 86 days. The last two days were a nightmare. My mind was thinking about "what now?" Who is going to help me make decisions? I felt alone. Yes, I had three daughters, eight grandkids, and other family members, but I was alone.

The first month, I was too busy to grieve because my daughters and I were responsible for handling the funeral and the numerous things related to the funeral. I realized what a wife has to go through when her husband dies, and I felt sorry for every woman who has that job. My daughters had a metal made with her fingerprint on one side and Joanne's handwritten name on the backside. The metal was fastened on a chain, and each grandchild wore it at the funeral.

Keeping busy was first on my bucket list because working on these tasks would make me tired and fall asleep faster. I had been working on a book about my teaching and was in no hurry to finish. Joanne would tell me to get it done because she would not complete the work if I died, and all my work would be wasted. I finished that book – "Memoirs of a Shop Teacher"– and saw the first copy a week before the anniversary of Joanne's death on October 11, 2020.

I tried to keep busy and push the emptiness aside, but my mind kept returning to Joanne. The thought of telling the world of Joanne kept returning. She would say to me, "never mind." but she had a life of giving to others, and I want people to know that.

This book is about Joanne; these words are for her. The idea was to start initially, proceed to October 11, 2019, and travel to the end. There will be copies of our letters written when I was in the Army, inserts from different people at her retirement party, family members, and even Joanne herself.

How did it happen? How did Joanne and Stan fall in love?

How did Joanne and Stan fall in love? My love started when I saw her as she opened the door for our blind date. From that day in 1955 to October 11, 2019, we were a couple, just boyfriend–girlfriend at first, then Husband and Wife. It was a journey made in heaven.

Joanne is not physically by my side, but I feel her helping me as she did for those 63 years. I can even imagine her telling me I did something wrong, like when I failed to pay a bill on time and had a penalty for late payment. I took it for granted she would be here longer than me. I know she didn't want to leave because she had several items on her bucket list. They were

1) have her hip fixed
2) see her grandchildren married.,
3) become a great-grandmother,
4) long walks on the beaches and
5) taking care of Stan.

How did our meeting develop into a good marriage? I thought about the stages we have experienced in the past 63 years.

1) <u>girlfriend or boyfriend</u>, all letters are lower case, no capital letters. We would say we just met a nice boy or girl. On our blind date and the next day, Sunday, when I met her parents and found out who "Stevie" was, we could say we met a nice girl or boy.
2) <u>"i like you"</u> all in lower case letters. After the first date, we spent time for several weekends and had time. I was with Jo when she was told she could not continue in the nursing program, and I helped her at a bad time. After a few weeks, we could say, "I like you" because we wanted to be with each other. It was fun.

3) <u>"I LIKE YOU!"</u> All capital letters. The change to capital happens one letter at a time, after a couple of months of meeting our families and participating in picnics and gatherings. We begin to feel closer. The conversations were more serious. I could see in the ways we looked and smiled at each other. I was a happy man. We wanted to do things together and saw how each other fit in with other family members' summer gatherings.

We enjoyed the family gathering.

4 "love" All lower case letters. When did I know I loved Joanne? I can't say it was a certain day. It seemed like as we went out on dates or talked on the phone, the feeling grew. Hearing the words "I love you" from another girl earlier (before I met Joanne) scared me. Joanne and I enjoyed each other as we went on dates, and the comments after we kissed changed, as did the hugs and words. Going home

after the date was not fun. I remember driving home to 123 Mustill Street and not remembering the drive home. Did I go through any red lights? I believe we both felt we could use the word "love" to describe our feelings for each other.

When I mentioned "I love you," it was sensational. My question was (a) would she like how I expressed my feelings or (b) put space between us because she didn't feel that way. She said she felt the same way and wondered if I liked her, too. The word meant so much to us. I found the woman I wanted. We talked about me going into the service because of my military obligation. "Marriage" was part of our conversation now. We didn't want to be married and separated. I had the ring and wondered when to ask her to marry me.

Christmas at my house 1955

Joanne caught Darleen Rennick's bouquet

Jo sitting on her front porch another "Action Shot." this
picture was taped to the inside of my wall locker

Joanne had the motion. She needs to practice more.
We are at a family picnic, "Action Shot."

Summer at Monroe Falls park summer of 1955

Both of us at Munroe Falls enjoying each other company

4) <u>"LOVE"</u> all capital letters. Here, too, the letters l-o-v-e changed one at a time. Leaving for the Army was an important decision because one or both of us could find another partner. After four months of letters back and forth, I decided to ask her to marry me when I gave her a ring. Things still could have changed, but the love grew. I began to feel we would be a team – husband and wife. Our tasks were to live each day until our wedding day, hoping our love for each other grew. The separation was hard for both of us, but I knew it would be best to complete this responsibility. This separation helped our commitment to each other. I remember looking for letters from her daily and writing almost every day as important as looking at the calendar for the day I leave the service or our wedding day.

5) <u>"marriage"</u> - lower case letters. Starting a family is not automatic; it takes work. We worked together in this new way of life. There were countless issues we both had to work on for this new team. Our beginning as a couple required a lot of adjustments common in marriage. We both worked at knowing how the other reacted to one's habits. Returning to work in the machining trade, I put in long hours, and my plans or ideas were now "our" ideas or agenda. Joanne talked me into attending Kent State University, and I had to develop confidence in this venture because I lacked confidence in my academic background. She helped me by working and wanting me to concentrate on my grades. Soon, I realized I could do this "college" thing

and graduated. I could work 30 to 40 hours my last year instead of Joanne working. I received a teaching position and now had to spend time working on my teaching materials. Homework was added to learning, and my time was spent at the kitchen table after the girls went to bed. Jo wanted to stay home with the girls, and we worked with my income to provide for them. We didn't go on vacations for several years because I worked during the summers. Our trips were to Cedar Point for the day. Joanne made clothes for the girls and enjoyed dressing them for the holidays. You could see her hovering over them at home and school and letting me worry about other things like providing income for our family.

In the later years, Joanne told me numerous times she was sorry she could not give me a son. I would look at her and tell her it was OK and not to worry. The reply was, "I have something to do with that too." I would say I had four sisters and no brothers, and God's plan for me is I will have three daughters. The son-like males in my life were in my classroom.

The lowercase word – "marriage" began to add a capital letter as we grew in love, and one year turned to two, and on to our 61 years.

6) "MARRIAGE" - all capitals. There was no exact day when marriage became all capital letters. The word MARRIAGE also changed from bronze to silver to gold letters in 61 years. I remember that our love seemed to be automatic and part of our DNA. We would stop and look at each other and reminisce about past times, both good and bad. Our embraces were there, but not the intensity and frequency of our early years. We always kissed good night, and there would be an occasional pat on the butt. Our routine became automatic because it had worked for years, and "don't fix it if it's not broken!" We had things to do and didn't think one of us would die. It happens, and now those things are still there, which may or may not get done. Yes! It's always that way. I think of things now I should have done and am sorry; I feel bad. I see Joanne's pictures and say out loud, "THANK YOU."

<u>From Hello to Goodbye?</u>

Our meeting on that blind date turned to love over three years. The first year, I was home, and the last two years, I was in the Army. The first year was typical of two people doing things that matched our personalities. She had to withdraw from the nursing program, and that was the first time she experienced failure. We only knew each other for five weeks. I think I helped her through that period and indicated my feelings for her. We met in early May; as the end of 1955 approached, we developed stronger feelings. At first, we "liked each other" in lowercase letters, and then we "LIKED EACH OTHER" in capital letters as the year ended. Love and marriage became terms after the beginning of 1956.

We decided not to be married until I fulfilled my six-year military obligation. I volunteered for the draft and entered the Army on August 20, 1956. We became engaged at the end of 1956, between Christmas and New Year's Day. I was in Arkansaw for nine weeks; for the last 21 months, I was at Fort Belvoir in Virginia, south of Washington DC. I could return on three-day passes and my 30 days of leave per year. The saying "absence makes the heart grow founder" was true. One or both of us could have found another but didn't.

Of the 730 days in the two years, we likely wrote 500 letters: I wrote more than Joanne. In each letter, we also had a few sentences indicating our love for each other. Joanne would write, "I hope you haven't changed your mind about me." I would always say silently, "no, no." I have included five letters to show how this feeling became stronger. I would say these three years before our marriage were perfect for me. Joanne or I could have found another person; I never thought about another person. I kept counting the days until my discharge day, August 19, 1958. We married five weeks before I left the service. With a 30-day` leave for the Wedding, I had to be without my wife for just 21 days.

Dating experience

Joanne told me she liked and dated several guys before we met. There was Jim D., a high school classmate at Cuyahoga Falls High School, and her prom date. She had a couple of dates with Harry, who drove an ambulance. I was next in her sequence of guys.

Joanne liked two other guys

Joanne didn't date these two but liked them a lot. She had a picture of one in our bedroom until I placed it in a drawer. I slept on the right side of the bed, and the picture was on a shelf. As Joanne looked at me, she could see Perry Como's picture. I would kid her: is she looking at me but seeing Perry? A talented Italian singer who had a regular TV program. I told her I would learn the words to some of his songs and sing for her; I got many comments and looks about that.

I took Joanne and her parents to a live Perry Como show at the Front Row, where the stage rotated. It was a good show, but I told her Perry's picture had to stay out of our bedroom or in the drawer.

The other "love" was Rocky Colavito, the handsome baseball player from the Cleveland Indians. I would kid her that I play baseball, too; why doesn't she look at me like she looks at him? Her biggest thrill was when we went to a doubleheader baseball game with Steve and Cathy Wronkovich and got tickets for the second game from a family leaving after the first game. We sat five rows behind the Cleveland dugout. Every time the inning changed, Joanne and Cathy Wronkovich would stand; as Rocky returned to the dugout, Joanne said, "he looked at me and smiled!". Cathy also "loved" Rocky. I said he was looking at those two women and was happy they had taken their <u>sons</u> (Steve and me) with them. Their replies were, we are just jealous. (NOTE) Joanne and Cathy were attractive women, and I'm sure Rocky looked at them and maybe smiled.

<u>Stan's few girlfriends</u>

I dated two girls, and I enjoyed their friendship. JG was my high school prom date, and we were friends off and on for three years. I made her a ring and engraved her name on the ring while I worked at Sackmanns. She attended a University, and I lost contact with her.

The second was DD, and we did things around the Christmas season in 1954. Our time together was typical of two people just meeting. She would say, "I love you," and I didn't know how to react. I am 19 years old and confused. That word seemed out of place in our activities. Love to me meant commitment, and I was unsure of this relationship.

When I was a senior, I guess you could call me shy. My parent started me in grade school when I was five, and I was usually younger than a high school student. At the start of my senior year, I was 16 and turned 17 on January 23; everyone else was 18 or older. I started working in the bowling alley when I was 13, a freshman at Hower Vocational High School, and worked at Sackmanns in 1951. My summers were full of baseball with a team that won championships four years in a row. I noticed girls when I bowled on Saturdays and the two girls who came to the baseball games, and I remembered helping a girl babysit when I was a junior.

Our First Date

After graduating from High School, I felt lonely because I didn't have those interactions in a school environment.

(note – When teaching, I commented to the seniors after their graduation, there will be times they will not have that daily interaction with fellow students and how they will fill that void)

The 40 + hours of work began to make me appreciate weekends. I was one of 6 – 7 guys who would meet Friday evening at "Kippys Restaurant" and be called "a Kippy cowboy," then do something else. We often went to a nearby restaurant and watched the Friday Night Fights from St. John's Arena in New York. I wanted that special feeling I had with my few girlfriends. I was ready for a serious relationship; I kept saying "no" to Steve's offer of a blind date. He assured me this was a nice girl, a friend of Dorothy's, his girlfriend, and my date was in the nursing program at City Hospital. I had not had a regular girlfriend or a date for a couple of months. Because we would play miniature golf, I said, "OK." I drove the three couples so my date would sit next to me, and Steve would sit in the front to keep the conversation going. Each guy drove their car to their date's house, and I would pick up the two couples and pick up my date last. We had trouble finding Joanne's house, but we arrived fine. I was nervous and anxious to see this young lady. The door opened before we reached the front steps, and I could see her for the first time. Silently, I said," She's pretty." We didn't enter the house; we just drove off. Joanne was close to me, with three in the front seat, and I was happy.

We all made the normal kidding and conversation about playing golf and what a nice evening with warm temperatures for early May. Steve made some comments that made me speak, which started my conversation with Joanne. It was about her classes, my work, and things that made the two of us talk and listen. Steve could not get a word in the conversation after a few minutes. The 15-minute drive to Hartville, Ohio, was quick. Joanne and I talked like we were old friends. We started to play like three separate pairs but soon became one group. Each couple had a scorecard, and Joanne and I wrote down numbers and did not comment about the numbers. I didn't care if she beat me. We enjoyed looking at each other and discussing how to play the shot best. I wanted this date to last because it was fun. We interact with Steve and Dorthy and Vince and Violet (they married a few years later). After the 18 holes, we drove to a restaurant for food and drinks. All the time, Joanne and I acted like we were old friends. The journey to her home was filled with laughter and nice comments about the enjoyed evening. It was Dorthy's than Violet's house, and now we are together, just the two of us. After Steve left, Joanne stayed next to me. I noticed and liked that. At 1785 E. Bailey Road, we arrive at the end of a great time; I open the car door and walk her to her front door; we walk in. Joanne had on a light jacket, took it off, and turned to place it in a closet. She opened the door, hung the jacket up, and turned towards me. I leaned over and gave her an ever-so-gentle kiss. It lasted about two seconds; I backed away and looked at her. She said she doesn't let guys kiss her on the first date. She didn't look upset. I replied there was always a first time for everything. I returned to my car and drove home feeling it was a great night. I had fun and met a nice girl; I was happy to say "yes" to this date. *NOTE: This is almost a repeat of what I wrote before. It was the most important event in our lives.*

Was She Ok With Me Kissing Her? Or Not!

I went to church on Sunday and was occupied with the idea of asking her if I could take her back to the dormitory on Sunday afternoon. God must have had this plan for us and helped me. It's called "Divine Intervention. She gave me her telephone number, playing golf. It would be nice if I could take her back. I called and thought if she were upset with me kissing her the night before, she would not let me take her back, but she said OK. (imagine seeing me saying "YES, YES" silently).

I arrived and met her parents and sister, Diana. As we talked, I noticed a picture of a lady I had seen catching a bus on Cuyahoga Street. I asked, "Who is this lady?" The reply was, that's my Aunt Delores. I said I knew her; I had seen her catching the bus, and my dad, who drives the bus, commented how nice she was. I noticed another picture and asked the same question. The reply was, "That's my Uncle Donald." I said I remembered he had a crazy-looking car. Joanne and her parents started asking me where I lived. When I explained that I lived on Mustill Street, the whole family talked about the Italian stores on Cuyahoga Street. They then told me they lived on Gotham Court until 1942 and then moved to Cuyahoga Falls.

We all were smiling and commented on what a small world it is. Joanne asked whatever happened to a little boy she used to play with named" Stevie?" I looked at her and replied, "STEVIE?" She said yes; he had two sisters who could not speak and lived on the other Street. I quickly replied, "Stevie," Steve Wronkovich fixed us up on the blind date. Everyone was surprised and excited. Joanne wanted to hurry and return to the dorm because Steve would be there with his girlfriend. She wanted to tell him she was the little five-year-old girl he used to play with in the neighborhood. I was happy being with her now and hearing what she had just discovered about Steve. I know I made a good impression with her parents.

When Steve heard that news back at the dorm, he spent the whole time with her asking questions, Steve's girlfriend and I talked about what he had just found out, and we had a nice time talking to each other.

How Joanne and Stan's Love lasted 61 years

The first date, first kiss, and meeting her parents the next day are events that started our lives for what it is today. As I reflect on the hundreds of experiences we shared with family and friends, those two events -one on Saturday and the other on Sunday- made me and us what we became in 65 years of being together.

I have to keep busy with Joanne's death on October 11, 2019, because it is hard to be in this house, and she is not here.

I considered writing about how Joanne and I developed this first date into 65 years together. I want to record our days, weeks, and years as a couple. She was a wonderful person. How she treated me and everybody else, how everybody would now have a chance to understand her, and why I loved her so much. In my heart, I felt her love too.

The blind date occurred on the first weekend in May 1955. It is safe to say we both enjoyed the date. I say that because she let me take her back to the dormitory. If she had said "no" and made the call short, I may not have seen her again, but she said yes.

We got together each weekend in May, and I would take her back to the dorm again. I don't remember calling her during the week because she studied and went to bed early because their routine was strict. When we were together, the date ended with, I think, at least one little kiss, but it was not sneaky.

Another Friday, we played tennis on the courts next to the dorm. The conversation was about Dorothy and Joanne playing a tennis match against Steve and me. Naturally, we took them up on the offer, but Steve and I had to practice because Steve lacked tennis experience. We both went to the courts by the Akron City Zoo and "practiced." It was like the blind leading the blind. We decided to make sure we had money to pay because of our skill level. The girls played because it was part of their course requirements. We agreed the loser would buy food and drinks at the Waterloo Drive-in Restaurant. The big event arrived; The guys won, And off to the Drive-in. We ordered the usual hamburgers and drinks and found out the girls had no money or said they didn't have any. They had little purses; we tried to grab and open them, but the girls got out of the car and started yelling and running away. We ran after them, but they kept screaming and running between cars. When the girls put their purses inside their tops, we decided that was "No man's land" and stopped. Steve and I said we had better stop because there could be someone who thought we were bad guys; we stopped and returned to the car. One thought was to drive away and leave the girls there; we forgot that idea. We told the girls they owe us dinner sometime in the future. We would not let the girls pay for the food, but it was fun telling them we would order the biggest sandwiches and double drinks.

On another weekend, the student nurses arranged a picnic at a metropolitan park on a Saturday evening, with food, music, and games. It was chilly, and couples were wrapped up in blankets, standing around a fire.

Joanne and I attended the University of Akron May Day Dance at Meyers Lake in late May. I found a little booklet that listed the May Day Queen and her Court. Joanne listed my name, and we danced and enjoyed the evening with others at the gala.

Joanne received her grades, and she failed the chemistry class and could not continue until she received a passing grade in chemistry. Jo knew she had trouble with the course because she did not take the class in high school. One option was to take a summer remedial class and take the year again. Everyone was consoling her because she was upset.

We talked about her not receiving passing grades for the nursing program. It bothered her emotionally because Joanne felt she was a failure in the nursing program. She was down in the dumps, and I said, let's go for a drive, just the two of us. Joanne sat next to me, and I enjoyed her touching me. I think she felt comfortable with me.

Bench Seats in the Old Car versus the new Car's and the Consoles

These experiences occurred in the 1950s, and one thing the guys enjoyed was the bench-front seats. The girls could sit close to the guy, touching each other. Today's cars have a console between the two people in the front, and it seems impossible for a girl to sit close like in the 1950s. I never had a car with a floor shifter, but I heard that was an experience for the guys. My cars had the shifter on the column, and after time and a few grinding experiences, Joanne and I could motor if I had my arm around her. The words were" palm down" to move to the third gear and "palm up" to go into second gear. My footwork was very important. I am sure the younger people are wondering what I am talking about; it's sitting close. Imagine the following story and imagine us in the car. I am driving, and she is sitting close.

We just drove. I didn't say much; I noticed a sign that said "Myers Lake," and we thought it would be nice to walk around. We heard music from the dance pavilion; we looked in, stepped in, and danced a few times. We were dancing close; I felt her holding me like she felt safe with me. My feelings were different; did she trust me? We only knew each other for a few weeks. I was trying to keep quiet and let her talk. Joanne felt bad because she thought she let her parents down, which was why she felt terrible. I wanted to reassure her that her parents did not feel bad because they knew she tried and continued talking about different plans she would discuss with her parents. Returning home, she and I (mostly her) continue to comment about getting a job. Her high school background was in office work.

<u>Joanne enters the world of work.</u>

She looked through the newspapers and noticed an ad for a secretary for doctor William Rogers, a pediatrician in Cuyahoga Falls. Her parents were very supportive, as was her sister Diane, and friends tried to cheer her up, but she was still very depressed. Doctor Rogers's job kept her busy, and now the emphasis was learning the Doctor's office routine of scheduling appointments and billing. She wasn't to be involved with the medical aspects of the nurse and began to enjoy that position. After all, she helped mothers with young children, which made her feel good because she was helping people with sick children, helping the Doctor be more efficient. She began to forget that she hadn't finished the program at Akron University. The job in the medical field helped reduce the hurt of not being a nurse. In time, she did many nurse duties and did the tasks well.

While adapting to working for Dr. Rogers and my working at Sackmann Stamp and Stencil Company, we are more involved with dating. We begin to do different things with friends and families. I made sure my mom, dad, and four sisters met her and included her in family activities. We enjoyed picnics and outdoor gatherings with both of our families. Her dad liked to take a Sunday drive to Ohio attractions to see the view; it was her mom, dad, Joanne, and me. Dianne had other plans. We began to like each other a lot more. I know I felt different about her, and I think she felt the same about me. Our comments to each other reflected those likes. We were both working and could only see each other on the weekends. We did use the telephone mid-week to plan our activity for the weekend.

I mentioned that I was one of 6 to 7 guys who would meet on Friday night at Kippy's, walk to the restaurant, and watch the Friday night fights. Each guy was to buy a round of drinks. I began to spend my Fridays with Joanne but occasionally be there. I was informed

I owed many rounds of drinks even if I was with Joanne. I was there in spirit. I said I would pay up at a future date.

Liberace

One Friday in August, we had no plans, just for me to come to her house. On the way home from work, I had to go to the Acme grocery store for my mom. That Friday a well-known musician performed that evening at the Akron Rubber Bowl, and Acme sponsored the performance. The performer was "Liberace." This gentleman was different; he was a gifted musician and a showman. Joanne and I weren't planning on going to the performance. The clerk at the check-out counter said she had free tickets to give if I wanted any. I said, "OK," and the clerk gave me four tickets. It's Friday at 5 PM, and the show is at 8 PM. I hurried home, called Joanne, and told her I got free tickets, and did she want to go? Her answer was "Yes." My mom hears me talk about the free tickets and asks if I have a ticket for her. I replied I had two extra tickets. My mom says I should ask Mrs. Braghieri because the older women like this guy. I hurry and call Joanne's house, and her mom answers and asks her if she wants to go because my mom is going. It was a quick "Yes." After the call, Joanne told me she was in their small bathroom washing her face when her mother came rushing in and told her to hurry up because she was going to. Joanne and I enjoyed watching the mothers more than Liberace. The mothers had a night out.

Liberace announced a special request from a couple to play a certain song because they would leave and elope after the song. I kid Joanne to get up, pretend we are that couple, and leave (but return). She doesn't want to shock her mom, and maybe my mom does too. Our moms enjoyed that night out, and it was free. One complaint was the bench was hard on their butts.

Meeting Her Old Boyfriend

I arrived at Joanne's house and noticed a sharp-looking car in the driveway. Joanne greets me at the door, wondering what I think or would do because her old boyfriend and two buddies came to say hello. I say OK and walk with her into the kitchen. She introduces me to the old boyfriend and his two friends. We ask each other questions, and they leave after some small talk. Does she wonder what I think? I tell her I bet your old boyfriend is mad at himself because you have another boyfriend – me. I am the lucky one now! Moments like this, we began to see how deep and sincere our caring was for each other.

Buying the Ring

I began working at Sackmanns after I completed my junior year at Hower. Mr. Klector, the Junior class instructor, asked me if I wanted to work in a shop, and my answer was sure. As the summer vacation ended, the company wanted me to continue. The company, school administration, and my parents agreed to allow me to coop. I would work in the morning till noon and then walk 400 feet to the school. I began full-time after I graduated in June 1952. In 1954, the company hired a man, Walter, who had a jewelry store in his home. As I began to brag about Joanne, they could sense my concern for her. I took Joanne to two fancy dinners; they knew her and thought a lot of her. The comments were like, "What does she see in you!" Walter talked to me and could see I was serious about Joanne. The time is mid-1955. We were very serious in our conversation. It was a big decision because our relationship could change. I decided to buy a ring and make weekly payments.

The finger size was a concern; how do I ask to see her ring (to place it on one of my fingers to determine the ring size) and not allow her to think about me buying her a diamond? I said I felt bad because I threw my graduation ring away playing catch with a cousin while on vacation in Rome, NY. I also checked out rings my sisters had (without them knowing why I was doing that). There were many beautiful rings, and I had difficulty picking out Joanne's "best" ring. I remember Walter said to think about the main diamond first and then the smaller stones. The ring was selected, and I began making payments each week. I rented a safety deposit box at Evans Saving Bank and placed it in the bank. I think I told my mom as long as she promised not to tell anyone. I would visit the safety deposit box several times to view the ring and walk away happy. Walter explained the diamond I chose was what he hoped I would pick.

The Dinner at the Smorgasburg Restaurant

Joanne was dressed up for this dinner
and made a big impression

Sackmanns would treat the employees twice a year to a fancy dinner at the Smorgasburg Restaurant in Stow, Ohio. I took my mom the first four times, and she was thrilled to go and disappointed when I took a girlfriend. After 1955, Joanne was my date, and she enjoyed this evening. The people could sense we enjoyed each other and complimented each other. At work, the secretary said, "She just fits in with you, and you both seem happy."; The feeling I had for her was increasing and turning into love.

<u>Visiting Joanne while in bed, not feeling well</u>

Our routine was to call during the week and visit on the weekends. I called on Friday, and Mrs. Braghieri told me Joanne was not feeling well and was in bed with a cough. I indicated I hoped she felt better and hung up. I sat there a few minutes, thought of her in bed, and decided to call and ask if I could sit with her and visit. Her mother mentioned I could catch what she had, but I said I would sit far away and keep her company. Even after Joanne yelled down, I could catch what she had; I said I would be careful. I arrived, went upstairs to her bedroom, and sat in a chair at the foot of the bed. We talked about different things and stayed there for about 2 hours – no holding hands or a goodbye kiss. I wanted her to know I cared for her and my plans were unimportant. After I left, she said her mom commented, "Stan must like you!" I felt good after those few hours with her. I remember a saying that one should see the person with a dirty face, in old clothes, happy, sad, upset, sweating, in bed, and after passing gas, and a couple I can't remember. Seeing her in bed with a cough and having to stay at the foot of the bed made me feel good. I thought I cheered her up a little, and I cheered myself up, too.

Entering The Army

<u>Joining the Army</u>

Young men in 1955 had a 6-year military obligation. If drafted, the man would have a two-year tour of duty with four years in the National Guard or Reserves. If the man joined, the time would be at least three years. Late in 1955, we discussed marriage; one issue was this obligation. The thought of being married and separated was a major topic. We discussed the possibility that one or both of us could find another person, which would lead to a divorce if married. We felt our feelings for each other would last and increase while in the service. It was like a test. This separation would make or break our love for each other. I would enter the military and marry after my time in the service.

I contacted the local draft board after the first of 1956 and asked what year and month they were sending draft notices. The answer was June of 1933. My birthday year is 1935. If we were to marry at age 21 (1956), I would have to leave her after a year or two of being married. We did not want to be separated. I heard a man could volunteer for the draft, and your name will be added to the next draft list. After much discussion, I agreed to request my name be moved to the next call. I entered the Army on August 20, 1956. We seriously discussed the long wait and set a September 1958 date for marriage. I had not proposed to her then, but we were obviously to be a couple.

August 20 was a Monday, and I had to be at the bus station at 8 AM. With 20 others, the trip to Cleveland for processing was fast and quiet for the guys. This trip was not like we were going to see a baseball game in Cleveland. We all boarded a train to Fort Chaffee in Arkansas. The entire contingent stayed together in the same company. We were "D-1-1" for nine weeks. Our time belonged to the military, but we still found time to write letters. The Akron contingent helped each other feel comfortable and informed each other of the news about Akron. My dad arranged for me to receive the Sunday paper a few days late. Others welcomed the daily paper late.

The thought of not being home for an unknown time was scary. I quickly wrote letters to Joanne and my parents. A mail call was made by a sergeant on a platform, calling names and throwing letters. He pauses and yells, "Lover Boy." Everyone laughs, including me. That guy will get a lot of kidding; It was ME! I was – "lover boy" because Joanne's letter did not have a stamp, and someone wrote Loverboy on the letter. I have 7 of the hundreds of letters we wrote, and the second letter Joanne wrote after the Lover Boy letter has her explaining why she forgot the stamp. Our letters express our feelings with the word "Love." I think of the saying "absence makes the heart grow fonder," which is a true statement for Joanne and me. Love appeared in every letter, and it solidified our relationship. When I was home with her, our conversation was like two people in love waiting for the day to become one in marriage. We had a small calendar that we sent back and forth. When I mailed the letter to her, I would continue marking off days, and she would do the same when she returned the calendar in a letter. We kept those calendars with little black marks crossing off days.

The words we used to remind each other of our feelings made looking forward to mail call each day. There were local news and sentences that made me want to return home. I did not sense any thought that maybe we should think of another person. She often wrote a sentence, and I remembered, "I hope you still feel the same way about me." My answer was "Yes, Yes," silently.

It seemed like a long time when I rode away from Akron to start the two years. Because my cousin Louis Bumgarner was in the same unit, we could talk almost every day. Louie was married, and his wife, Ruth, lived a few blocks from Joanne's house. The daily ritual kept me from thinking about home 24 hours each day. Days became weeks, and soon, we were in week nine, our last week. The graduation from basic training was exciting because we were to travel to another duty assignment. Most assignments included a 10 to 14-day leave and then the next duty station. I was excited because I was going home. I was called along with a friend, Floyd Hildebrand, and assigned to Fort Belvoir, near Alexandria, Virginia, south of Washington DC, but no leave. Our tickets were for a train ride to DC. After feeling bad about having no time home and Joanne, I thought I was close to home and maybe those three-day passes. Joanne and I felt bad, but we mentioned I was 300 miles from Akron and close to the Christmas holidays. I didn't receive the leave because of the holidays when I most likely would have time home. That decision was correct. I felt bad about not going home but realized it was a good move.

Floyd lived near Cincinnati. He asked how close the train would be to Cincinnati because he would tell his wife and family to be by the tracks and wave at him as we went by. We did not come close to his hometown.

The move from the fields of Arkansaw to Washington, DC, was a night and day difference. I was excited to see Washington for the first time, but it was just for a few hours. The bus came, and we traveled to Fort Belvoir for 21 months. The only way to talk to Joanne was by phone, and I had to have the charges reversed. I had no permanent assignment for a few days and made a few calls.

The time frame is the following. I entered the Army on August 20, 1956, and did basic training until November 2, and I arrived at Fort Belvoir on November 4. As a new arrival, I spent a week at a company waiting for further orders. I was assigned to the 580th Redstone Missile Company. Their mission was to provide fuel to the Redstone missile – Liquid Oxygen and Carbon Dioxide.

I now had an address and could receive letters, but I had no civilian clothes. The calls were few and far between. I wanted to come home to see Joanne; I had it bad.

The Crazy Trip Home Soon After I Arrived at Fort Belvoir

Walking to the mess hall, I noticed an Ohio license plate with the same combination of numbers and letters as we had in Summit County: one letter (usually A or B or C), three or four numbers, and another letter. The person who owns that car must be from my area.

Saturday afternoon, several guys and I were in the barracks. One guy said he would like to get some civilian clothes off duty. I asked him, "Where do you live?" He replied Youngstown, Ohio. I replied, "I live in Akron." He said do you want to go home? It's Saturday afternoon; the common sense answer should have been "no" because there is not enough time to drive the 300 miles home and back before Monday's morning formation. But I said yes, and we drove off at four o'clock Saturday. The roads from Belvoir are typical two-lane rodes until we arrive at the Pennsylvania Turnpike at the Breezewood interchange. I was to hitchhike to Akron, 40 miles away. I was in love, and getting home clouded my mind -"Love is blind." We arrived at the Youngstown interchange around 2:00 AM, 40 miles from home, wearing my Army uniform because I had no civilian clothes. I walked over to the side of the road, heading to Akron, holding out my thumb. The second car stopped and asked me where I was going. "Akron" was my answer. The guy said he was going to Akron, too. We talked about what I was doing; he questioned what I was doing regarding the chance to be AWOL (absent without leave). He had been in the service and said I was taking a chance. He must have been sorry for me because he drove to 123 Mustill St., my house, at about 4:00 AM. I knocked on the door and surprised everyone. I called Joanne and told her I was home for about ten hours because I had to return to Belvoir at that interchange. I changed into civilian clothes and drove over to see Joanne. Couples should see each other in a different situation, like early morning, when they are sleepy. I did see her, and she still looked good.

Albert was to work that Sunday from 6 AM to noon, and we took him to work. We parked and spent time making up for the last ten weeks we didn't see each other.

How can we get back to that interchange by the time John set? My Uncle Johnny said he would take me back because he had a new car. There was a plan for two cars to drive me there if one taking me had problems. We got there, Joanne hugged and said goodbye again - Off to Belvoir.

We left Belvoir at four o'clock Saturday afternoon, drove till early Sunday morning, and got up all day. We met at the Turnpike interchange at four PM Sunday afternoon to return and be back before eight AM Monday morning. The turnpike drive was quick, and John took a nap. Now, we have that two-lane road with twists and turns following the hills and mountains in Virginia. Fatigue arrived for both of us, and we drove two hours at a time. I, at times, opened the window and stuck my head out the window to stay awake. I was afraid. We arrived at Belvoir around 4:am and lay down for two hours. We got up, did what was expected, and slept very soundly that night. Before I went to sleep, I called home to tell them we had arrived with no problems. John and I talked about this trip and how crazy it was for us.

Letters

We wrote letters almost every day during those 720 days. I probably wrote more than Joanne. My mom chews me out for not writing, so I decided to write at least once a week. I will include four letters to illustrate our feelings for each other. We both realized the other one could meet someone and break off the relationship. That was the main reason I joined before we married. I would make a copy of the original letter and include it. Julia, my granddaughter, said including the letters will show your love for each other, but some people may not read cursive writing. So, type the words in the original letter and include the letter. That will be what we did for the three letters. I typed the exact words, sentences, and punctuation we used then; we made mistakes, but we didn't care.

Letter # 1 August 31, 1956. Entered the Army
August 20, 1956, was the second letter.

Gosh was it hot here today around 85°-90° and my office is like an oven. I suppose now we will have horrible weather for the holidays. Oh well such is life. I just came home (9:35 PM) from billing. Dr. Rogers is going out of town tomorrow & Mon, so I will finish the bills tomorrow so I won't have to do any at night; enough of my troubles.

Gosh I bet you were so embarrassed when they called out about the letter. Don't think the Army will get you some extra privileges like free postage, huh? Oh well now they'll be on the lookout for you again "Lover." I received two letters today. I hope by now you're gotten my notes, or at least one of them. You write wonderful, interesting & your spelling is OK. Keep it up. I tried to get hold of the ma but could only get 3 home. Yes she told me that you missed me very much& when I heard this I cried. Honest I felt so very bad. Please write in enough time for me to know to stay home. I love you very much.

Isn't charting a plane expensive. Gee it would be nice, but I think the Army puts you fellows on a train &sees that you get on. That's correct I think because Frank had to do that.

Joyce is fine. She came in the office the other day & said her dr. told her she could do anything, even drive a car. So she said she'd be able to take my vacation job. Well that's if she doesn't get something else. Remember me telling you about my grandfather. Well he had a malignant tumor (cancer) on his hand & the Dr, said if they would left it alone in 2 mo. Time he would have his whole arm cut off. Boy take care of yourself dear

Don't let the guys kid you too much about me. I'll have some more "action pictures" taken & send them OK!

Hope your details are not too hard. Our song is slowly disappearing from the radio; maybe we can get another someday when you are home & we can listen together! OK? I hope you haven't changed your mind about me.

I saw Steve & got all my junk & badminton set back but I haven't seen him or anyone since.

I can have 2 years to learn how to cook I know I can do it for you. When your home I" ll surprise you with a whole meal fixed just by me.!OK? I know I'll except the lifetime job if you offer it ≥ (means within medical shorthand). I got carried away. Excuse me please sweety.

Tomorrow night is Billies' Wedding & Marilyn & I are going. I'll try to write when I get home because its over at 10:30. By the time I get Mar home it will be around 11:00 so I can still drop a line To my favorite soldier boy!! Be good now & obey your commands (ha, ha) OK. Write soon. I will too. Be my little boy always! please. Mom says "Hello" she just yelled it at me. Dad has the fights on now. Oh well I think I will go to bed & get some sleep. Its raining now & lightning a little. Well don't get discouraged try real hard. With all my love & all my kisses (X) "Love ya" Sweet dream, hope I'm in some of them Always yours Joanne

August 31, 1956

Hi Stan,

Gosh was it hot here today, around 85°-90° and my office is like an oven. I suppose now we will have horrible weather for the Holiday. Oh well such as life. I just came home (9:35 pm) from billing. Dr. Rogers is going out of town tomorrow & Mon. so I will finish the bills tomorrow so I won't have to do any at night. Enough of my troubles.

Gosh I bet you were so embarrassed when they called you out about the letters. Don't think the army will get you some extra privledges like free postage huh? Oh well now they'll be on the lookout for you again "Lover." I received 2 letters today. I hope by now you've gotten my letters, or at least one of them. You write wonderful, interesting

Probably the 2nd letter. Entered the army Aug 20, 1956

25

& your spelling is O.K. Keep it up.

I tried to get ahold of the no but could only get 3 homes. Yes she told me that you missed me very much & when I heard this I cried. Honest I felt so very bad. Please write in enough time for me to know to stay home. I love you very much.

Isn't chartering a plane expensive. Gee it would be nice but I think the army puts you fellows on a train & see that you get on. Thats correct I think because Frank had to do it.

Joyce is fine. She came in the office the other day & said her Dr. told her she could do anything, even drive a car. So she said she'd be able to take my vacation job. Well

3/ that is if she doesn't get something
else. Remember me telling you about
my grandfather. Well he had a
malignant tumor (cancer) on his hand
& the Dr. told him if they would have
left it alone in 2 mo. time he would
have to have his whole arm cut off.
Boy take care of yourself you hear.
Don't let the guys kid you too
much about me. I'll have some more
"action pictures" taken & send them. OK?
~~Hope your details are not to hard.~~
Our song is slowly disappearing from
the radio maybe we can get another some
day when your home & we can listen
together, OK? I hope you haven't changed your
mind about me. I saw Steve & got all my jugs
& badminton set back but I haven't seen
him or anyone since.

& I have 2 yrs to learn how to cook & I know I can do it for you. When your home I'll surprise you & a whole meal fixed just by me! OK? I know I'll except the life time job if you offer it. = means within medical shorthand I got carried away. Excuse me please sweetie. Tomorrow night is Billie wedding! Marilyn & I are going. I'll try & write when I get home because its now at 10:30. By the time I get meg home it will be around 11:00 so I can still drop a line to my favorite soldier boy!! Be good now & obey your commands (He He) OK. Write soon. I will too. Be my little boy always! please. Mom says "Hello." She just yelled it to me! Dad has the fights on now. Oh well I think I go to bed & get some sleep. Its raining now & lightning a little. Well don't get to discouraged try real hard. With all my love & all my kisses ⊗ "Love you" Sweet dreams. Hope I'm in some of them. Always yours, Josephine

We were kidding my mom about being short

This Was The Letter From December 31, 1956

I was in the Army for four months and stationed at Fort Belvoir.

Hi My Stan,

Hope you are feeling OK and not to worn out. Stan, don't ever forget this "I Love You." You don't know how much. I'd love to kiss you now and hold you so very tight like last night. Your dad took me home & Betty and Arlene came home with me. We played Monopoly all afternoon. Your Mom and Dad & Helene came over (I asked them after you left). If I couldn't be with my Stan I could be with someone close to him. My mom and dad talked & laughed with your family. They really looked happy I wish you could have seen them; it made me feel very lost without you. Well one more day than 1957- It won't be too long. I can hardly wait till "58.

This is only going to be a short one. Will make up for it tomorrow. You never told me how I should get my hair fixed for the picture. I don't think I'll have it in time for your birthday. Boy, are you getting old - me too I know.

My ring looks very beautiful but now I have some tears in my eyes & it's blurry. I felt horrible seeing you off Stan I've tried to be brave so hard someday. I'm going to get you from that train or bus & keep you all for myself. Write to me soon. Be good and careful for I want you home the same as you left. I could never love you more than I do now. - I'm yours

PS (front page) Don't be sorry for anything Stan I loved every second of your leave it was wonderful – Happy New Year (X)

Joanne all my love is yours

28-Nov-Thur.

Hi My Love ⊗

How are you this Thanksgiving?
Fine I hope. We had turkey for
dinner but it wasn't as good
as my mom's. It is also raining
with a overcast sky. I called
home and talked to my aunt
and Uncle and my parents. My
Dad told me that Bowser lost
8-0. Well there is next year. Even if Bowser
does play I won't go because
I'll have to help with the
dinner. (???) Rita said they tryed
to call your house but there
was no answer. I figure you
and your parents went to
Cleveland to see cinerama
Is it "The 7 wonders of the world?"

You don't have to say anything about it because I've heard a lot about it from some of the fellows in the barracks. I hope you enjoyed it. I was up at 9:30 and got a haircut from some fellow in the barracks. Whitsell another fellow and myself went for a cup of coffee and arrived back in time to play a couple hands of cards. We had dinner and after dinner I helped Whit prepare for guard duty. I then went to St Martin's and said a rosary. I then called my parents. The Texas & Texas A.M. football game is now on and I watched some of this real good game.

It's not 9:30PM and almost time for lights out. I made mistake of spelling your last name on the envelope. I was concentrate on printing your name real neal and forgot the "R". I ~~was~~ worked on my English for a couple of hours this evening. there is a 250 theme to write, then I will be able to type and send the lesson in completed. Today seems so much like a Sunday. We had left-over for evening supper. What did your mom have for your main meal? I went to town on the assorted mixed nuts they had at the noon meal. I brought some back in a cup and been ~~so~~ nibbling on them all day. Maybe you'll ~~this~~ ware mixed nuts when you become ~~pregnant~~ pregnant. Time will tell.

I had you on my mind a lot today. Thinking of my next Thanksgiving, were I'll be, what I will eat ~~etc~~. Sometime during the day next Thanksgiving I want to go to church and give thanks for all that I have. If I have you my prays will have been answered and this is the ~~reason~~ for ~~giving~~ thanks.

It's late my love, be ~~the~~ mine, I ~~too~~ be seeing you soon. Don't forget that I'm still your little boy. I remain as always Yours
forever Stan

P.S. I love you very much Joanne. Please wait a few more days (260) and help me to wait. I saw some maps with colored handles. What color do you like? (I'm kidding)

34

<u>This Is From June 1, 1957,</u> Ten Months in The Army

Hi my little boy(X)

In your letter today you sounded real good. I guess the school is helping out real well. I'm very glad it is me? I'm very tired & not feeling like myself. I don't know what's wrong. I couldn't sleep last night & today I've just felt terrible. Rita & I didn't go anywhere because of it. It's a terrible night too, very rainy. One of those nights when you and I can be alone with just the records playing. In your letter today you said you may try & make it home next weekend. It sure would be nice but I'm not counting on it too much because I'm getting used to that Army business. You know what I mean.

You are a better printer than I am. You know what Stan I don't have ½ of the bills out & what's more, I don't care. Isn't that terrible. I'll go in Mon, Tue & Wed eve & get them done but I just didn't feel like it today.

Yes we are in the month of brides but Sept sounds real nice especially if you promise to keep me warm & not pull all the covers off!! If you do, mind you, I'll make you sleep on the floor next to SSS jr. You have to behave or else. You have to mind your mother. Well we are down to 444 today. I'm getting tired of 4's soon I can write 3's. Well Stan I'm going to try & get some sleep now. Goodnight, sleep tight & pleasant dreams too Stan. Oh yes, I still want you for my little boy no one can love you any more than I love you Stan. Be mine forever; I'm yours forever – Joanne(X) (X) (X) I miss you more than ever its hard to say goodnight(X) (X)

PS Leonard Gmerich' wife had a baby boy named him Leonard too. She had a rough time with it. Her mother called Dr. Rogers to see the baby

P.S. Don't be sorry
for anything Stan I loved every second of your   Sunday December 31
leave it was wonderful — Happy New Year!
Hi my Stan,

Hope you are feeling OK & not too
worn out. Stan don't ever forget this
"I Love You". You don't know how much
I'd love to kiss you now & told you so
very tight like last night.

You dad took me home & Betty &
Arlene came home with me. We played
monopoly all afternoon. You mom & Dad
& Helene came over (I asked them after
you left). If I couldn't be with my
Stan I could be with someone close
to him. My mom & dad talked & laughed
with your family. They really looked
happy. I wish you could have seen
them it made me feel very lost

without you. Well one more day & then 1957 — It won't be too long. I can hardly wait till '58.

This is only going to be a short one. will make up for it tomorrow. You never told me how I should get my hair fixed for the picture. I don't think I'll have it in time for your birthday. Boy are you getting old — me too I know.

My ring looks very beautiful but now I have some tears in my eyes & its blurry. I felt horrible seeing you off Stan I've tried to be brave so hard some day I'm going to get you from that train or bus & keep you all for myself. Write to me soon. Be good & careful for I want you home the same as you left. I could never love you more than I do now. Will write more later — I'm yours Joanne
all my love is yours.

This is halfway through the two years – November 2, 1957

Hi My Love (X)

How are you? As I sit here I vow that I'll be with you 52 Saturdays from tonight to celebrate your birthday my way. I know it'll probably be November 3, but the Saturday night celebration will be just you and me. OK? The public celebration will be on the 2nd. Today I got up and Whit and I went down to the PX. They have those panties sets. They have different colors for each day. I would like to buy you a set but will wait, I am thinking of your wedding present from me and I have a lot of ideas. This gift will be very personal. Do you have any idea of what you want? Maybe we are thinking too much too soon. Ask my mom for my sister's sizes. I also bought a number painting set, rather, Whit and I did. We have a picture each. It's a cocker spaniel. I'm going to St. Martins to confession and then to call you.

Bye for a (X) a little while

Well here I am back in the barracks. After I hung up from my call to you, I walked back very slow and felt good in that I had talked to you and was glad that You were feeling better.

Right now there about 4 fellows in the barracks including me. From 8:45 PM to 10:00 PM I was the only one and was it peaceful and quiet. All I want is a diamond needle and a lot of 33 1/3 LPs and naturally You. From 8:45 to 10:00 I worked on my number painting doggie. You are right when You said that once You start a picture you don't want to quit until You finish. I have just one NO. done. I saw some wastepaper baskets which are paint by numbers. I bought a Christmas present for your father with about 9 more presents to go. Enclosed is that money order, also a cartoon. Which do you like better?

I was sort of choked up as I was about to hang up, and I think you were to. Who have you told about our changing ---- wedding dates? Your father? sister? anyone in my family? I have it real bad and not ashamed of it in fact will tell everyone I can. (x) I love (X) You (X) very(X) much (X) Joanne (X). I'm (X) yours (X) forever

Stan(X)

PS I hope I see you real soon. Thanks for saying Yes to my June proposal. We'll make it the best thing anywhere. I'm still your little boy. OK?

P.S. Leonard Gmerick wife had
a baby boy named him Leonard Saturday June 1st '57
with it. Her mother called wanted too. She had a rough time
Hi my little boy ⊗ Dr. Rogers & see the baby.

    In your letter today you sounded
real good. I guess the school is helping
out real well. I'm very glad it is.
Me? I'm very tired & not feeling like
myself. I don't know whats wrong. I
couldn't sleep last night & today I've
just felt terrible. Rita & I didn't
go anywhere because of it. Its a terrible
night too, very rainny. One of those
nights when you & I can be alone with
just the records playing. In your letter
today you said you may try & make it
home next week-end. It sure would be
nice but I'm not counting on it too
much because I'm getting used to that

Army business. You know what I mean.

You are a better printer than I am. You know what Stan I don't have ½ of the bill out & whats more I don't care. Isn't that terrible. I'll go in Mon, Tues, Wed eve & get them done but I just didn't feel like it today.

Yes we are in the month of brides but Sept sounds real nice especially if you promise to keep me warm & not pull all the covers off!! If you do, mind you, I'll make you sleep on the floor next to Std Jr. You have to behave or else. You have to mind your mother. Well we are down to 444 today. I'm getting tired of 4's soon I can write 3's. Well Stan I'm going to try & get some sleep now. Goodnight, sleep tight & pleasant dreams too Stan. Oh yes, I still want you for my little boy no one can love you any more than I love you Stan. Be mine forever. I'm yours forever – Joanne Ⓧ Ⓧ Ⓧ Ⓧ I miss you more than ever. Its hard to say goodnight Ⓧ Ⓧ

This Was The Next To Last Letter August 5, 1958,

Hi My Love (X)

How's my girl today? Fine I pray. Me" I'm in real good spirits because I'm a short-short-timer with 13 days & a wake up as of today (Tuesday the 5th) If you receive this on Fri. the 8th I'll have 10 days and a wake up. There is just one more Tue, Wed, Thur, & Fri apart for us. Mrs. Sipka we have it almost beat. Thank you for staying with me and helping me through the last 720 days.

Joanne they have me on guard duty on the 15th which will include part of Sat. and KP on the 17th a Sunday. I won't pull these duties and explain why: A post regulation states that the company and section must release the individual 3 working days before their ETS date. (E-T-S= end tour of service) Saturday and Sunday don't count as working days, so... Wednesday the 13th is supposed to be my last day for company duty and final day in the lox area. Now if you are going to come to Belvoir to see your old man let me know Sunday when I call. Did you ask your mom and parents about coming down?

The rest of this week we will be busy GI ing the barracks because it's inspection time for Company I. I am short enough to miss it but I have my wall & foot lockers shaped up in case I have to stand the inspection. Turner gets out September 4 and he has to stand them. I don't harass him too much. He may stop in Akron on his way home in Sept. Whit is also going home in Sept and may stop on his way back.

Hilderbrand came in this evening with his processing papers in his hand. He just received them and is released on the 20th.

Well my love it's almost 11 PM and past my bedtime. I didn't receive any mail today. Maybe something tomorrow. Well Jo we have only 8more letters to write if you don't come down and only5 if you do come down. Here's the last Money order. You should have 5 in all.

If I'll call Sunday between 8 – 9 PM. I hope this is our last long distance phone call. It feels good to write our last this & that the last time. It's been a long time.

I am your loving husband Stan (X)

<u>PS</u> I (X) love (X) you (X) very (X) much (X) Joanne (X). It'll be nice being your little boy every nite again, but it'll be very much nicer to be your husband. I'll wait and I know you can too. I hope I have made our being "one" something. You look forward too instead of ???????. We have a lot to do yet and I'll do my part to make you a happy woman. I'll try really hard too.

York MOTEL
6287 PEARL ROAD
CLEVELAND 30, OHIO
Telephone TU 4-8302

8 MILES SOUTHWEST OF DOWNTOWN CLEVELAND ON U. S. ROUTE 42
5 MILES NORTH OF TURNPIKE

5-Aug-Tue

Hi My Love (X)

How's my girl today? Fine
I pray. Me? I'm in real good spirits
because I'm a short-short-timer
with 13 days & one a wake up as of
today (Tuesday the 5th) If You receive
this on Fri the 8th I'll have 10 days and
a wake up. There just one more
Tue, Wed, Thur & Fri apart for us;
Mrs. Sipka we have it almost beat.
Thank You for staying with me
and helping me through the last
700 days.

Joanie they have me on guard
duty the 15th which will include
part of Sat. and KP on the 17th
a Sunday. I won't pull this

duty and I'll explain why: There is a post regulation which states that the company and section must ~~let~~ the ~~endiva~~ individual ~~~~ 3 working days before his E.T.S. date. (E-T-S = end tour of service). Saturdays and Sundays don't count as working day so... Wed the 13th is suppose to be my last day for company duty also my last day in the L.A. area. Now if You are going to come to Belvoir to see your old man let me know Sunday when I call. Did You ask your mom or parents about coming down?

The rest of this week we will be busy ETing the barracks because it's inspection time for Company I. I'm short enough to miss it but I have my wall & foot locker shaped up in case I have to stand the inspection. Turner gets out Sept the 4th and

8 MILES SOUTHWEST OF DOWNTOWN CLEVELAND ON U. S. ROUTE 42
5 MILES NORTH OF TURNPIKE

he has to stand them. I don't harass him too much. He may stop in Akron on his way home in Sept. Whit is also going home in Sept and may stop on his way back.

Helderbran came in this evening all smiles with his processing papers in his hand. He just received them. He is released the 30th.

Well my love it almost 11 PM and past my bed time. I didn't receive any mail today. Maybe something tomorrow. Well Jo we have only 8 more letters to

write if you don't come down
and only 5 if You do come
down. Here's the last money order.
You should have 5 in all.

I'll call Sunday between
8-9 PM. I hope this is our last
long distant phone call. It feels
good to write our last this & our
last that. It's been a long time.

I am your loving Husband
Stan ⊗

P.S.
⊗ I Love You⊗ Very⊗ Much Joanne.
It'll be nice being your little
boy every nite again but it'll
be very much nicer to be your
husband. I'll wait and I believe
You can too. I hope I have made
our being "one⊗" something You look
forward too instead of despising.
We have a lot to do yet and I'll
do my part to make You a happy
woman. I'll try really hard too.

The Day I Proposed

I don't remember the exact day I used the words "Will You Marry Me." I thought it was Christmas Eve 1956; it must have been during the week. We met in early May 1955, and I propose one and one-half years later.

I paid for the ring in 1955 before entering the Army and placed it in a safety deposit box. I came home on a seven-day leave and planned to give her the ring. I arrived at her house and sat on the couch waiting for Joanne; we planned to go to a movie. No one was in the living room; I placed the little black box behind the couch out of sight. We returned; she went upstairs. Her parents and sister were in bed. I took the ring, placed it on my little finger, and twisted it around with the diamond out of sight. Months before, I gave her a "temporary" ring with the Fort Belvoir logo, and she was wearing it on the finger, waiting for the "real ring." She returned, and we were close and talking about the evening. I made some excuse about the ring leaving a mark around her finger that I had to take it back. She would not let me and said it was hers. After struggling, I removed the ring, asked, "Will You Marry Me?" and slipped the diamond on the finger. She didn't realize it was the diamond. She looked down and saw the stone instead of the Belvoir logo and let out a yell, "YES." We embraced, and I realized what I had just said and her answer. Of course, that was the answer I expected, but hearing her say "yes" couldn't be imagined. Our words were different from then on. I would not hear "I hope you haven't changed your mind about me!" in many of the hundreds of letters I received.

She kept looking at it, and then we would embrace; it was a different feeling. She said, "Who can I call?" I mentioned it was near midnight. The goodnight kiss at the door felt different. I realized my life would change from now on. That was a night in December 1957; it's now 2021. What a journey!

After being engaged, my conversation changed; now, we plan on being a family. Family members on both sides looked at us differently because we would become part of their family. People shook my hand, and I received a lot of kidding. I enjoyed it immensely. Those four words, "Will you marry me!" were magical. I felt relieved because I was sure Joanne wanted me to ask her, but only the word "YES!" was what I wanted to hear.

Sunday, we went to Church at St. Joseph Catholic Church, and I looked around, thinking this would be where we get married, but when will that day be? We visited my family and others announcing the engagement but didn't have a wedding date. Before entering the Army, we talked about our wedding date after leaving the service on August 20, 1958. Our general plan was a September wedding. My parents were married on July 7, and her parents on June 30. We had several dates around these dates, but we checked with the church and their calendar. We traveled to St. Joseph's rectory, talked to the secretary, and looked at the calendar for June 1958.

The two times, 9 AM and 11 AM for June 28, were open. We thanked the lady, went to Joanne's house to discuss the times, and decided the 11 AM Mass would be good. We called to schedule the 11 AM time and were told the 11 AM time was just booked; We had to take the 9 AM time. We found out the secretary had written her granddaughter's name at 11 AM after leaving the office. I remember the other wedding party wanted to share the cost of some flowers. We didn't agree to that. What happened? After the Mass, our crowd socialized in front of the church; Both sides of the family had many guests. They enjoyed talking after the Mass and didn't know there was another wedding (note - we heard about this after, but we didn't feel bad). The new crowd had to maneuver through our family members. When the other wedding party arrived, we were still talking and socializing. We had a lot of family and friends in attendance. We also had many cars in the church parking lot and heard many other wedding guests' comments about the distance to walk to the church.

Planning the Wedding

We asked for and received the 9 AM Mass on June 28. The Italian hall was ours after we made the down payment. We were relieved that important details of our wedding were completed, but now, for the numerous seemingly little details,

A soldier has 30 days of leave for each year of service. The importance of not being given a 14-day leave after basic training was a good thing. I had leave time for my second year, and we scheduled a 30-day leave for the Wedding, seven days before June 28 and 23 days after the Wedding. I would return to Belvoir and have 30 days remaining until discharged.

Joanne worked many hours for Dr. Rogers but loved working on features regarding the Wedding. I arranged three seven-day leaves to help, but she did most of the work to have a perfect wedding day. Joanne, her family, and the wedding party developed a list, and each item was included or rejected; her wedding party took care of one thing at a time. She talked about finding her gown and the excitement of trying on different dresses, veils, a negligee, shoes, and stockings. The guys had to get fitted for a tux and matching shoes.

My days home were filled with working on wedding details like a honeymoon hotel, drinks, and a band. Still, the girls seem to have more lady things, like the caterer, menu, drinks, wedding cake maker, photographer, wedding announcements, newspaper articles, and wedding party members; who should you invite? What kind of tux for the guys? It was a busy time, and we loved every minute. Our letters and frequent calls were full of "what do you think?" comments. Our Wedding would have been the first for both families, and we realized we could have too many people, and listing the names and not including some was hard to do. Day by day, June 28 approached, and we completed our details.

Joann placed her picture in the Akron Beacon Journal announcing the engagement and was bombarded with telephone calls for items for newlyweds. She arranged for a salesperson to visit to show pots and pans because he promised to give her a nice gift for allowing him to make the presentation. He went through the presentation and then announced the price. Joanne said she would discuss it with me, and I was in the Army. He said he would get back and prepared to leave but didn't give Joanne the items she would receive. Jo's dad got upset because he and Julia were listening but let Joanne decide. The man said the gift was if she purchased the set. I was told about the cost. I said we should wait, and we did.

On Saturday, June 21, I returned home a week before the Wedding and started the 30-day leave. (NOTE – the first Sargent allowed me to "sign out" two days earlier) The leave started on Monday, June 24. There was the marriage license, tux fittings, and a haircut for me. The ladies had all kinds of details to schedule. I had to get my fingernails "fixed" for a picture of us holding hands for our wedding album. The lady looked at my hands and said, maybe I should place my hand on the bottom with Joanne's hand on top to cover my nails. In other words, my fingernails were not good for the picture. Joanne had the week off and needed the free time to go with me to the places to check on details. We did not let others do what we wanted for our Wedding. We did not have a formal rehearsal dinner after the rehearsal in the church. It was most likely sandwiches at Joanne's house.

Both families were busy preparing for the company after the Mass and before the evening reception. The Mass at nine and reception at 6:00 allowed six hours filled with activity for our out-of-town guests. After pictures at the downtown studio, the plan was to have Joanne and the ladies stay and rest at Joanne's house, and the guy stayed and relaxed at my parents' house. The afternoon at both homes was busy with activities. It was like a small family reunion for my mom's Rome, New York family.

It was busy, and we loved every minute.

Drinks – Almost Going To Jail

Our Wedding was typical: a church ceremony in the morning, a big reception in the evening with a sit-down dinner, band, liquor, and dancing.

I took the job of planning and obtaining the alcohol and drinks. I could purchase liquor at Fort Belvoir at the PX (Post Exchange) at a reduced price. On my 3- three days pass, I would buy three bottles, bring them home, and store them for the Wedding.

On the last day of 1957, December 31, I did something that could have sent me to jail, and my life today would have been different. I was never so happy to see one soldier wake up on New Year's Day morning, January 1, 1958.

I had three bottles in my footlocker this New Year's Eve, ready to take home the weekend after New Year's Day. There were four guys in the barracks, including me. A new guy was in the barracks and found out I had some liquor and asked if he could buy a bottle. I sold him a bottle. Another guy and I sat around talking while this guy started drinking whiskey like most guys would drink pop. He went out and came back an hour later with an empty bottle. He was very agitated and started to turn over bunks footlockers and yell. The other guy and I tried to stop him, but he was out of control. The idea of a cold shower was next; we turned the four shower heads with COLD water and pushed him to the back of the shower, hitting the four showers and going in and out. We stopped him and did the routine again three times. Finally, he seemed to settle down, so we took him back to his bunk, and he went to sleep.

The two of us walked away but kept an eye on him, and we thought it was OK, so we relaxed. He awoke again and ran outside. We put on our shoes and ran after him, but he disappeared. We looked for several minutes around the barracks and then under the barrack. We found him sleeping next to a column. We carried him back, put him in his bunk, tied him in, and stood there for several minutes. He struggled against the covers, yelling, throwing up, and urinating, and then became quiet. I stood there much longer than the other guy to ensure he was asleep.

The guy who helped me said I should get rid of the bottle because this guy could die from drinking so much so fast. To hear the word "DIE" scared me. He went to sleep, and I watched him as long as possible. I hid the empty bottle in my locker, wondering if I should wipe my fingerprints from the bottle and throw it away in a different trash container down the Street. My bunk was across the aisle and down a few beds. I woke up, and the first thing was to go over and talk to him. He moved and started to speak and realized what he was lying in, which made him sick. The kid didn't remember anything and felt bad for a few days. I was scared this young guy would die from drinking so much, so fast.

I would have been sent to jail, dishonorably discharged, and other things that would have affected my life. So, I stopped buying liquor at Fort Belvoir.

Our Wedding on June 28, 1958

"JUST MARRIED"

June 28, 1958, Saturday was a beautiful sunshiny day. Joanne and Stan became husband and wife at a 9:00 mass at St. Joseph Catholic Church in Cuyahoga Falls, Ohio. I was in a room adjacent to the sacristy, waiting and watching the ushers escorting people to their seats. Then, the church begins to fill with family and friends. Joanne's mom is escorted to her seat in the front row. The priest and I walked to the front of the altar; now, I was nervous. The music was playing, and people turned to watch each bridesmaid slowly meet her partner. Standing there, I could not see Joanne at the end of the aisle. Then, the music changes, people stand, and I can see Joanne and her father slowly walking down the aisle. What a sight. She was beautiful. I almost said, "hurry up!".

Taking her hand was the start of the journey I wanted with her. As we repeated the words, we looked at each other, and everything changed as two became one. Father McCausland then looked at us and said: I now pronounce you, "husband and wife!" Looking at each other was a lasting memory. The Mass ended; the walkout with Joanne on my arm was too quick. The first kiss out of the church was like the first one on the blind date. The next kiss lasted longer. Outside the church, we met our combined new families and didn't realize the crowd we had. We drove around, the horns sounding, and we just looked at each other. On many dates, I would ask if I could stay with her tonight. She replied, "no, you have to go home tonight!" She said she sometimes wanted to say "yes," but we had to wait. Joanne looked at me as we drove around and said, "You don't have to go home tonight!" My reply was, "Good!"

The Mass ended at 10:30; we arrived at Joanne's parents for sandwiches and drinks. The ushers opened a bottle of whiskey, and we had a toast to my life with Joanne. I held my glass, touched the other glasses, and downed the drink. Then, one of the guys started to fill the glasses again. I stopped and put my glass down. I thought two or more drinks could make my Wedding a disaster.

We drove downtown, had pictures taken, and returned. Because the reception was at 6:00, and it was now 2:00, the ladies would stay at Joanne's house, and the guys would drive to my house to rest. So I took off my tux, played catch with some of my cousins, and did rest a little.

My side of the family went to my house, where it was like a Rome, N.Y. reunion. Family cars were parked down Mustill St because of the crowd. My Uncle John (from Rome, New York) had his suitcase stolen; he could have bought a suit from my dad. Food was available at both houses, and our guests from out of town had a place to relax until the evening reception. I remember there were a lot of people there.

Joanne at home showing the beauty of the dress

Niagara Trip   Akron Beacon Journal **7B**
                         Sunday, July 13, 1958

Joanne Braghieri Wed To Stanley S. Sipka

Joanne Christine Braghieri and Stanley S. Sipka were married in St. Joseph Catholic Church by the Rev. Joseph E. McCausland.

The bride is the daughter of Mr. and Mrs. Albert Braghieri, 1785 Bailey rd., Cuyahoga Falls. The groom is the son of Mr. and Mrs. Stanley J. Sipka, 123 Mustill st.

The bride's gown was of silk taffeta and Chantilly lace, designed with fitted bodice and long tapered sleeves. Lace appliques embroidered in seed pearls and iridescent sequins trimmed the portrait neckline.

★

The full skirt of lace and taffeta extended into a cathedral train. The veil of matching lace and taffeta pill-box was trimmed in seed pearls and attached to a fingertip veil of silk illusion hand rolled. She carried white carnations, stephanotis and a white orchid with her rosary.

Diane Braghieri, sister of the bride, was maid of honor. Bridesmaids were Phyllis Falkenstein, Betty Sipka and Rita Sipka.

Steve Wronkovich was best man. Ushers weer Vince Capizzi, Bob Klingingsmith and Jack Sipka.

★

The bride was graduated from Cuyahoga Falls High School and is employed by William B. Rogers, M.D.

The groom was graduated from Hower Vocational High School and is stationed with the Army at Fort Belvoir, Va.

The reception was held in the Carovillese Hall. From that event the couple left for Niagara Falls. They will reside at 1785 Bailey rd.

MRS. STANLEY SIPKA
—Irving

newspaper article

Our Wedding Day would start with the 9 am Mass and the evening reception. We wanted the 11 am mass time, but the church's secretary didn't let us have that time. We both got up around 6 am to prepare for this day. The plan was to rest a few hours after pictures and arrive at 6 pm to start the reception. To be there and see Joanne again, now as my wife, was a great feeling. We sat and ate the meal; tables were removed and prepared for the evening. We both were involved with the traditional things at our wedding. There were dances with parents and grandparents and the wedding party. Joanne had a grandfather and grandmother there, and I had a grandmother. We cut the cake and agreed we would not do anything funny with each feeding each other a piece of the cake. The garter and bouquet were tossed outside in the front of the hall. We made sure we talked, even briefly, to each person to thank them for coming. The band consisted of six guys who would take turns dancing with the good-looking girls in the bridal party. We met the people at a reception line and toasted each guest, but our drink was ginger ale. This was no time to drink liquor. The photographer helped with the time for the different things we wanted to do and not be around till midnight. NOTE – I knew the band leader, and we would meet later; he would comment about the good time he and the guys had, and the girls were "Sharp!" We had a good time, and someone asked me how long we would stay at the wedding. The wedding dance started, and Joanne danced with those in line and ended up dancing with her father. We left the hall and drove to Joanne's parents' house. As we drove over the gouge bridge, I realized I wasn't going home by myself anymore. We were married. We looked at each other and realized this was our beginning. The first kiss long ago was the best thing I had done. For us! The best was yet to come.

Honeymoon

We searched for a place close to Cuyahoga Falls because we knew the cost, and the car we were to use was a 1950 Ford. Joanne used this car to drive to work, and we thought 30 to 50 miles away would be fine. Flying to a distant location was not part of our plans due to the cost. I was receiving almost nothing each month, and Joanne was the only source of income. We drove to the York Motel in Parma, Ohio, and made reservations months before.

We were both involved with our Wedding's standard features: the dinner, reception line, bridal dance, dancing with parents and grandparents, and meeting everyone to say hello. We talked before; we wanted to greet everyone, even if it was a few sentences. We threw the garter and bride's bouquet, and Joanne danced with individuals who put money in a bag. We took that bag, thinking we might need the money. I believe it is called the money dance. Finally, we left and went to her parents' house; it dawned on me that I was not going home that night. My mind was not back at the hall!

We arrived at the house and went to different bedrooms. I went to Diane's, and Joanne went to her parents' room. I am hurrying when Joanne calls for help. I walk in, and she needs help with the many buttons on the back of the dress. Being a good new husband, I do the job and return to finish dressing. She calls me again to help her take the dress off. It wasn't easy to take the dress because it was full. I place the dress on the bed and turn to see Joanne. She says, "See what we have to wear!" Now I see a lot of skin and think I better get out of this room because we have an hour's drive to Parma and a week to see that skin. Joanne's mom packed and hid our suitcase because we heard "our friends" plan to mess with our clothes. We also thought those friends would follow us to the motel.

In one of Joanne's early letters, she mentioned she saw a negligee and thought of buying it but changed her mind. She would wait until near our day. On the night of our wedding, she wore a negligee. She came out of the bathroom, turned slowly, and looked at me, asking, "How do you like it!". I said it was beautiful, and other words, I asked her to remove the outer cape. The gown she had on was sheer – very sheer. I sat on the bed and looked as she turned around slowly; after less than a minute, that piece came off, too. As the week progressed, she commented that she might have saved the money by buying the negligee because it hadn't worn very long. That was my favorite outfit for years. The hours were eventful, and we slept happily next to each other. Our wait was over. Now, our life was beginning. We acknowledged our wedding gift to each other was we saved our virginity till our Wedding.

We went to a noon mass; as we left for the mass, I informed the desk that the air-conditioner unit was noisy. After mass and before eating, I was going to get the camera. She stayed in the car, and I entered the room and walked to a closet to get the camera. It wasn't there; I looked around, and our clothes and that bag of money were gone. The room was clean, like no one used the room. I thought we had been cleaned out; everything was gone. I even checked to see if I was in the right room. The room is on the second floor, and Joanne can see me walking around and wondering what happened. I saw two ladies cleaning the rooms and asked them what had happened in our room. One lady said they moved us to another room because of the air-conditioner. Both of us laughed about what we thought occurred, and maybe it was our friends who messed with us.

We drove to the Cleveland airport to buy some postcards to send our friends, and we wrote that we were waiting for our plane to take us to some fancy place. Most knew we were kidding. We noticed information about the Cleveland Zoo and planned a short visit there on Monday.

We spent the time at the zoo holding hands and walking with no problems. The touch of our hands and looking at each other made a simple day relaxing after the busy weekend. It was not crowded; it was like the zoo was there just for us to enjoy. While there, we noticed pamphlets for the ship "Aquarama." We took one and decided to take a "cruise on Lake Erie" the next day.

The ship had multiple decks and could have cars drive on, and the vessel would travel to Detroit and return. We could now say we went on a "cruise." Again, the time sitting on the various decks and enjoying the time together doing something unplanned. They had a restaurant for the noon meal and returned to Cleveland. Our conversation mentioned we were on the west end of Lake Erie, and on the east end was Niagra Falls. Joanne asked questions about Niagra Falls, and we decided to go to the famous honeymoon site for years.

I had not been to the Falls but passed close by on our trips to Rome, New York. It would be a four-hour drive and could be a one-day trip on Interstate Route 90. We started on RT. 90 and noticed the car was heating up, so we moved to Route 20. I was familiar with this route. On the way, we saw places advertising rooms and tours. We stopped and booked a room and tour. After we drove away, we wondered if we would be sorry. We visualized the tour bus with hundreds of people and a room with bugs. We had a map (remember, no GPS or cell phones) and were told the motel would be after an airport and on the road's left side. It began to rain hard, and we entered Canada. We are driving and looking for the airport on the left side. We did see an airport, but it was on the right side. We stopped and figured out we were going the wrong way. We found the motel on the opposite side of the road. The motel was nice and had no bugs. We commented that we went to a foreign country and Niagra Falls and wondered how bad the tour bus would be.

We are sitting there waiting for the bus when a limousine pulls up. The driver stands by the car, and we go out and ask if this is our tour bus. He said yes, and another couple came out, and we drove out to see the Falls. There were just two couples on tour. The other couple were not on their honeymoon and were from Brooklyn, New York. We had a six-hour tour, and it was enjoyed. We drove back to Parma, happy we traveled to a foreign country and the Falls.

We stayed at the motel on Friday and Saturday, our last day. We checked our money and ate at McDonald's and White Castle. Then, we could take two chairs on the balcony and talk about our future. We didn't want the week to end, but it ended, and we returned to Bailey Road on Sunday Morning. Look out, world, here we come!!!!

We drove to the 11 o'clock mass at St Joseph and arrived home after the Mass. The plan was to have an "open wedding present afternoon." We received a lot of gifts and were careful to record who gave us the gift.

The honeymoon is over, and now, the daily routine of being a husband and wife is over. Now, the two of us had to think like one. What was in our future? We must make the lowercase word – "marriage" turn into all capital letters, and we made it happen.

My Return To The Army For Four Weeks

I had 21 days after the Wedding to adjust to living with Joanne and her parents and sister. I didn't have a car, but Joanne had a 1950 Ford (our Honeymoon car) with many miles. I even think Joanne had an extra week off to make those changes with her name change. I kidded her I would go with her when she returns to Dr. Roger's and be the custodian. The day arrived to return, and knowing this would be the last bus ride to D.C. was nice. I had 29 days until the discharge day. We agreed I should not return during that time. That was hard for me to make, but I knew there would be no more days away from her. I was a <u>Husband</u> with a <u>Wife</u> ready to plan our lives for lord knows how long. Those familiar places where the bus stopped, many early mornings, would soon be a memory.

I showed the guys pictures of the Wedding and Joanne and enjoyed the comments about Joanne. Guys asked questions about where we would live jobs, and many seemed concerned about our futures.

Soldiers are classified as "short-timers" when they have 14 days until release. Because of discharge processing, the soldier must not be on guard duty and K.P. within the last five days. The weekend does not count in those five days.

August 19 was a Tuesday, and I planned to return home with my cousin, Louie Bumgarner, who was with me two years ago when we left Akron. He had a car, and there was room for our belongings.

Joanne and Family Coming to Fort Belvoir

I would be discharged on Tuesday, August 19, and return home with Louis Bumgardner. Joanne and I talked about her coming to Belvoir and the three of us returning on D-Day. However, plans changed because Joanne's parents, sister Dianna and my sister Betty were to visit the weekend before D-Day and then return with Joanne staying with me and returning on Tuesday.

A week before that Tuesday, I went to the hospital with a rectum problem; It was a fissure. Wednesday, I was on the operating table, bent over and groggy from the spinal and other drugs. It was no big deal to me. The instructions were to stay in bed for 12 hours because of the spinal. I waited the 12 hours to the minute, walked the 150 feet to a phone, called Joanne, and told her what had happened. She became excited because she knew this was not a simple procedure. As we talked, I began to feel like I would pass out and had to hang up. I just returned and got hell from the nurse for walking to the phone. She told me I would have a rough time with headaches for a while.

I scheduled three rooms at Fort Belvoir's guest house Friday, Saturday, and Sunday, and one room till Tuesday for Joanne and me. Joanne and her family arrived Friday night, visited the Base, and retired to our rooms. During the night, I had a dreadful headache and could not stand the pain. Joanne used her dad's car and took me back to the hospital. Joanne had no idea how to return to the guest house. She asked an M.P., and he helped her find the guest house. They visited me in my hospital garments on Saturday, and I could not show them Washington, D.C. Louie and Lloyd Whitsell guided them around Saturday.

Joanne brought our new camera, and Louie and Lloyd knew their way around D.C. and took many pictures. I returned home and noticed we had a couple of pictures to take until we developed the film. The little dog was the subject of two photos. I went into a closet, rolled the film back to the start, opened the back, reached in, and discovered no film in the camera. We laughed and said we would have to visit someday and ensure we have film in the camera.

I thought I would be kept in the hospital after August 19 because of my condition, so Joanne returned to Cuyahoga Falls with her parents. I recovered and returned home with Louie on the 19th. Imagine how we felt finishing our two years and heading home! The car was filled with a lot of smiles.

Joanne and Her Work

Joanne adapted to the routine at Dr. Rogers and was an asset to his practice. The job helped her put the nursing program to the side. The disappointment was always there but slowly disappearing. She learned her job, and mothers appreciated how she helped with appointments and general information. She could provide basic information when mothers called and were in a panic. I remember Joanne and the Doctor staying past 5:00 because of a special problem. She had favorite mothers and some who were not. There were times she instructed new mothers who knew she would help. A couple of nurses stayed for a year or two, which was easy on Joanne.

Billing was a duty that took a lot of time. There were no computers; she wrote each bill, affixed the stamp and mail, and recorded payments, although an outside accountant made the final statements.

How She Spent Time

On August 20, 1956, I entered the Army and was not engaged. My time belonged to the Army, and Joanne worked and lived with her parents and helped take care of her grandma, who lived next door. Jo's high school classmates were close friends and shared many events. I remember her telling me about a "club" called "The Tulies" for girls only and secret - no boys. I never did find any "secret" about the club, even after 61 years of marriage. She would talk about going with different girlfriends and family gatherings in her letters. The family drove to California to visit her Aunt in September of 1956. One evening, several friends came to her house and talked to her because I didn't write to those guys. She wrote and told me how her whole family talked about what I was doing. I knew she was in the real world and would find out if there was another person for her. One of us could have found another person and told the other the relationship would end.

Trouble in Marriages (not our's)

Several guys received "Dear John" letters, and I watched and listened to them. One guy lived in Oklahoma and was set to leave on a 30-day leave. His friends found out his wife would issue him divorce papers when he arrived home. They arranged for him to arrive at a different airport and hide him away from his wife. She wanted everything, and he didn't want that to happen. He secretly contacted a lawyer, had papers made up to counter her demands, and flew back to Belvoir. He then contacted her, presented her with his demands, and mentioned he planned to enlist for six more years. She wanted out of the marriage and agreed. My friend was happy.

Another guy received a letter from his fiancée, which messed him up a little, but the guys and a minister helped him through the time.

"Shorty" received an emergency notice from home to leave for home ASAP. There was no word why. "Just get home." We were all concerned for Shorty. He went home to West Virginia and returned three or four days later. He joked about why he was called home by his father-in-law. His wife had two younger brothers who found a picture of Shorty with a girl taken when he was in high school. The brothers sent the Father a letter with a note that this was Shorty with a girl in D.C. The father was ready to shoot Shorty for hurting his daughter when he saw Shorty, but the father asked him first about the picture before shooting him. He quickly told the father-in-law it was an old picture and didn't know who had sent it. The father found out his sons sent the picture as a joke. Shorty said he talked fast, and those two sons were almost shot.

Joanne, After Working for Dr. Rogers

Joanne was a medical assistant, and soon after working for Dr. Rogers, she joined the local Medical Assistants Organization. She became the recording secretary, knew all the members, and provided the monthly meeting notes, which kept her busy. Jo sent monthly bulletins to the members, attended the officers' meetings, and attended holiday parties. When she was dismissed or fired from her job by Dr. Rogers, the members found out and rallied around her. She had many offers from others for her to fill in for vacations. She substituted for two or three weeks of leave and was constantly asked to fill in. The pay was equal to or more than what Dr. Rogers paid. She also learned how easy the work was at some doctor's offices. Jo mentioned she had finished a task and asked the doctor if she had another. "It was never like that at Dr. Roger's!" was her reply. Joanne started working for Dr. Rogers in July 1955 and worked for doctors until 1962. She became pregnant in early 1963, and we moved into our house around Easter that year.

How She Helped Families

Joanne was the one who scheduled appointments for the mothers and their children at Dr. Rogers's office and prepared the patient for the nurse and Doctor to examine. Her working hours were from 8:00 am to 5:00 pm five days a week. You will see times when her workdays went past five o'clock in a couple of her letters. She would try accommodating the mothers because they were concerned for their children. Dr. Rogers had a busy practice and was liked by many. There were days when the mother would be allowed to bring in the child near the five o'clock hours, almost certain which would lengthen the workday. We would often be somewhere and meet a mother who would greet Joanne and thank her for squeezing them in before five. She also begins to perform some duties that the nurse could do, like giving shots.

<u>Out of the Service – Living at her house</u>

I am out of the service, married, and live at her parent's house. We had talked about living in an apartment. The plan was to wait and not be in a hurry. I returned to Sackmanns, and Joanne had been with Dr. Rogers since July 1955. One thing Joanne did was save most of her pay while I was in the Army. She was concerned about money then and every day of our marriage. Our Wedding was to happen, and there would be expenses. Her parents showed and encouraged her how to save, and she did.

My hours were from 7 am to 5 pm five days and 4 to 6 hours on Saturdays. Joanne's parents said we should take our time looking for a place, and they would not charge us anything for rent. They wanted us to save our money. We had an idea when we would move out and wanted to make sure it was the correct move. We looked at places, talked to our friends about their arrangements, and considered buying a house.

We received a call from my Uncle Happy during the week to come over (Frank Starr, married to my dad's sister); they lived in Tallmadge. We arrived and sat by the kitchen table and talked about various things. My Uncle said he had an important thing to ask us. How much would we pay for the lot next to their house? We were startled and commented that we had no idea about the land cost, so we kept indicating that we could not reply. Finally, he said, "OK, would you buy it for $300?" Again, neither of us could say anything; we did not know what to say. Finally, Uncle Happy said, "OK, would you buy it for $250?" We were quiet, and our facial expressions indicated we were dumbfounded. We looked at him and my Aunt and could not say anything; we were silent. He said there were a couple of conditions placed on the offer. One, we would have to build a house and not sell the land. Two, we would have to take care of Aunt Helen if she needed it. We were not to answer then, but we went home and gave the offer much thought. Uncle Happy presented that to a family member on his side of the family, and that couple said "no." We were not to answer now, but take time and give it a lot of thought. It is important to Aunt Helen.

Did we hear that right? A lot worth thousands, and we could buy it for $250. We mentioned this to her mom and dad at Joanne's parent's house. They, too, were surprised at what we just said. The cost was the first thing we discussed, followed by the implications of being caregivers for Aunt Helen. The evening was full of issues about the second part of the offer. What happens if Aunt Helen dies first? If Uncle Happy dies first, which he expected, how long could Aunt Helen need help? Joanne's grandmother lived next to them on Bailey Road, and Julia was expected to care for Grandma. It was a lot of work for Julia. The biggest item was if Aunt Helen lived, Joanne would have the biggest responsibility, not Stan. It was like the burden would be on Joanne to help Aunt Helen and our kids. Would that be fair to Joanne? We were offered a question mark deal that could last years and be bad. We talked until it was time for bed and promised to speak tomorrow. The land was not the talking point.

We went to bed and asked ourselves if we heard what Uncle Happy said was right. It was like a dream offer but could become a bad dream. Each evening, the four of us talked about the proposal. Joanne's mom and Dad did not tell us to "do this or do that." Did they mention that caring for a bedridden person can be nearly impossible, and would that be fair to the kids? We talked to my parents, too, and they had questions for us to consider. What were we to decide?

One of Joanne's best features was caring for people. Her desire to become a nurse and work for a doctor showed her willingness to help people. She helped her mom care for her grandma, who needed help later in life. I could not tell her she had to care for Aunt Helen; that would not be right. When she insisted we should say yes to my Uncle's offer, I kept telling her I didn't want to commit her to maybe a time-consuming promise. I could not do those women's things for my Aunt, which would be hers to do, maybe for months or years. She said we would have a place to live – A HOUSE. Those were the magic words.

We told my Uncle, "Yes," we would do both items he asked of us. So we drove home happy, and now we had to look for house plans. No, not yet.

Kent State University - the need for more education

Having a lot in Tallmadge, we would build a house at 508 Southeast Avenue. The address was there before the house. My Uncle told us we should wait because the City of Tallmadge was planning to install water and sewers, which could happen within a year. We are just married; I work at Main Mold and Machine Company, and Joanne works for Dr. Rogers and lives with Joanne's parents.

I began to feel I needed more education. First, I tried a local for-profit school, but they would not let me test out of the basic classes I had in High School. We were looking for an apartment, and I took courses at night. Joanne said I should try Kent State University for one year. Mr. Donavan's decision to help was important. The work at Main Mold was making plastic injection molds for local companies. The experience there was another important aspect of my teaching; the skills acquired were a major part of my presentations in the machine trades program.

Joanne said I should try Kent State University. My answer was a quick "no" because I attended Hower Vocational High School, and the courses were not college-oriented. I was afraid not to work and spend time in College.

The days we talked about college were the most important in our marriage. We could not foresee how Jo's encouraging me made our life. I was afraid. I spoke to Mr. Andy Donavan, Owner of Main Mold and Machine, who encouraged me to work when my schedule allowed me time. I worked 8 to 10 hours during my first year, usually on Saturdays. After that, my hours increased to 40 + in the fifth year.

The plan was to attend KSU. I would not be working with little or no income; the idea of living in an apartment was set aside for the time. We would make plans to live in the basement. There was a stove, refrigerator, table with two chairs, a couch, and washer and dryer in the other half of the basement. Joanne's dad and I constructed a sink and counter. I felt I was making their life difficult, but Joanne's dad wanted to fix the basement with a kitchen and "living room" for our use. He enjoyed helping. We had a small Christmas tree and decorations; One wall had a lake and mountains scene mural. We put floor-length curtains next to the picture. It was our window looking at the mountains.

We used the room every day like an apartment. We cooked, washed the dishes, and enjoyed the little time we had for ourselves. We did not stay upstairs. Instead, we purchased a desk and lamp to help with completing assignments. Joanne typed even though I could type, but not as fast. Joanne would go upstairs to watch T.V., and I would watch it on weekends. We kept to ourselves and enjoyed the space. We enjoyed playing music, sitting on the couch, and discussing our future. It was mood music, soft and slow; the L.P. (long playing) records would play for hours.

KSU

My experience with college was before I met Joanne. I attended a class at Akron University in 1955 and took an introduction to algebra class. I received a grade of "C." In 1959, I was 24 years old and felt like a senior citizen in the orientation class at KSU. The goal was to be an elementary teacher and a coach. The psychology, English, and math classes were frightening, and Joanne helped assure me I could do the work. She was so helpful and so patient. The desk and typewriter were busy in the basement working on assignments. I was a nervous wreck waiting for the grades. The grade was 2.4 for the 12 hours, and we celebrated at a restaurant. Joanne said I could do this, and that made me feel better.

The second quarter was a 2.6 grade. Near the end of the third quarter, I was returning home; it began to rain. I walked through Van Dusen Hall, which I never entered. I noticed a room full of machine shop equipment like I used at Hower. I asked the instructor about the machines and wanted the "Industrial Arts Program." The next few days, I changed my major to Industrial Arts.

While checking out the I.A. program, I also learned the details of the Vocational Educational program. My journeyman classification was the vocational program's main feature, and I attended Hower Vocational High School. The idea that I could teach at Hower was a new goal; I had a double major by the end of my first year. The first year began, and I was scared, and it ended with definite goals.

Miscarriage

It was June 1960, and I had just completed my first year at KSU. I was happy with my progress and felt more confident I could continue. Joanne discovers she is pregnant. We wanted to be sure before we announced the news. One morning, she awoke and was bleeding; we rushed to the hospital, and there was a miscarriage. She must rest at home and not return to work until the Doctor clears her. The time she is home is filled with concern about her ability to carry a baby. Julia had two daughters and two miscarriages. Each pregnancy, Julia was bedridden from complications. Joanne began to wonder if she would be like her mother. I worked during the summer, and Joanne returned to Dr. Rogers's office.

Joanne Is Laid Off

We resume our routine her with the Doctor and me at KSU. Joanne becomes pregnant around March of 1961, has trouble with morning sickness, and can not return to work. Julia tells her this was how she was when she was pregnant. The projected day for birth is early January 1962. Joyce worked for Dr. Rogers before Joanne and substituted for Joanne. In the third month of the pregnancy, Joyce tells the Doctor she wants the full job time. The Doctor tells Joanne he has to give Joyce the job and is sorry. Joanne is crushed. No one knows how long Joanne will be bedridden; it could last for nine months or one more month. It was one more month. She began to eat and feel good after the baby moved (that's what they said), and we all ensured we helped her take care of herself.

Our daily routine was going to Kent and working a couple more hours, and Jo was not working and taking it easy. Our bedroom was on the second floor, and our "apartment was in the basement." So Joanne stayed on the main floor and avoided going up or downstairs. (The time is the middle months of 1962).

Christine

With a due date of early January, I decided to take 18 credits (three 5-hour classes and one 3-hour class in the fall quarter and a small class load after the baby arrives.

Joanne is feeling better, and the routine is to wait until the end of this year. On November 17, Friday night, she, the others, and I watched the Steve Allen Show near 11 o'clock (Steve Allen's show was like Johnny Carson or Jay Leno). Joanne's mom is in St. Thomas Hospital and will return home on Saturday. Albert, Joanne's dad, goes to bed because he has to get up at five o'clock to work at the B.F.Goodrich Company. Albert leaves the house, crosses the Street, and catches the bus. Just before 6 am, Joanne woke me up very upset because "her water broke." She tells me we have six more weeks to go for the projected birth: this is too early. During this time, families were given a pocket-size book to read during the nine months. I didn't read it, but I was going to after my classes were over in two or three weeks. She asks what it says about what to do when the water breaks? I grab the book, open the book, and land on the page that explains what to do. That was divine intervention. The baby's guardian angel opened the book for me. We called the Doctor and rushed Joanne to the hospital. At about 8:30, the Doctor tells me we have a girl who weighs 3 pounds 9 oz. I sat down and thought about what I had just heard. I am a Father, and Joanne is a Mother. She was moved from one room to another and passed by me. I walked over, and we kissed, and she expressed concern about the weight. The baby's features were beautiful. What now?

I am standing there thinking about what I should do. Julia is upstairs, waiting to come home. Albert is at work until noon, and it's my dad's birthday. I went upstairs to tell Julia but stopped outside her room, wondering what I should say about the baby. A nurse asked if she could help me, and I explained the situation. She suggests Julia not be told at this time and wait until she is to leave the hospital. Good thinking. I drove down the Street looking for Albert and found him waiting for the bus. He was concerned but quickly smiled when he heard the good news. We returned to the hospital to see the baby, but not Julia. We drove home so Albert could drive his car to take Julia home while I stayed with Joanne. Julia was told she could not see the baby because she was a surgical patient, and those patients couldn't visit the maternity ward. Julia was upset, but an older nurse would take care of this problem for Julia. She was taken to the exit in a wheelchair, got out, is now an outpatient, returned as a visitor, and went to see Joanne and the baby. The nurse winked at Julia, saying, "We did it!"

I called my mom and told her we got my dad his birthday present. She said to wrap it up and bring it over for the birthday party tonight. I said we couldn't make it because Joanne just had a baby for Dad's birthday present. Joanne had many visitors; my dad said that was the nicest birthday present he could ever receive.

Christine stayed in the hospital until December 14, when she weighed five pounds. Joanne and Julia were told not to visit the hospital because of their recovery, making them upset. A student nurse - Sue Fisher - would call Jo daily and tell the baby's progress. That made Jo feel better. Albert and I were there every day at night.

Christine stayed in the hospital until she weighed 5 pounds. The Doctor told Joanne not to travel to the hospital. She was not happy about that, but she listened.

Joanne would not take the baby out to show relatives and friends because Christine was pre-mature, and Dr. Waickmann, our pediatrician, told us to avoid crowds because the baby was so small at birth. We let people know we were concerned; they understood.

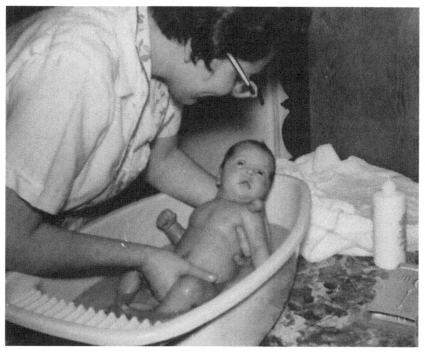

Christine is getting a bath on the kitchen table,
looking at "mom" and saying, "Don't drop me!"

Three weeks later, my sister Rita gave birth to twins -Michael and Michele. Then, in January, My sister Betty gave birth to Darlene. Thus, my parents had four grandchildren in three months.

The House Plans

January 01, 1962, I was finishing my second year and completing the core courses. The IA courses were to be a major load after the end of this year. The Vocational Educational (VE) classes were at night. My work at Main Mold increased, and that helped with our income. Living at Joanne's parents' house was what allowed this to happen. Joanne's main goal was Christine and typing for me; the assignments were more involved.

Joanne would bring down the baby in the morning and use the dining room, now a nursery. The new grandmother – Julia, enjoyed this addition to the house.

Joanne and I would talk about building the house on Southeast Ave. in Tallmadge and realize that dream was getting closer by the day. We would buy books about homes and plan what we would like in our home. We had a size restriction because the lot was 72 feet wide but 532 feet deep. As we drove around, we would notice brick houses and look at one-story dwellings. A big factor was that Tallmadge had installed water and sewer lines on the street.

We had to add a playpen in the living room because Chris was crawling and walking. We removed the baby crib from the dining room and replaced the table and chairs. It's Thanksgiving, and all five of us are sitting down for the meal. Joanne fed Chris and placed her in the playpen. She is sitting there enjoying her toys. We are there for a few minutes when we hear her crying differently. We all rush in and see Chris in and out of the playpen. The pen had wood slats. We can see her head in the pen with her body outside. She squeezed through the slats, but her head was too big. We pushed her back in, and someone held her while we finished the dinner. There were some changes to the pen after that.

Student Teaching

In September of 1963, I started my student teaching at Sill Middle School, and we had to watch our pennies because I could only work on Saturdays. Christine was two years old, and we lived at 508 Southeast Ave., and Joanne was pregnant.

Sill was close to our house and overcrowded. My supervising teacher was Mr. William Watts. He was 35 years of age and had been teaching for ten years. I was his first student teacher. I worked my way to leading the classes quickly and was happy with my experience. After a couple of weeks, Mr. Watts and Mr. Elmerick, the Principal, and I had a meeting. They asked me if I wanted to take one-half of the eighth-grade class to a classroom and teach mechanical drawing. This would cut the eighth-grade last-period class into two groups, and the classes would rotate in my class and the shop. I said OK because I knew what I was asked to do. Mr. Elmerick would visit the class twice a week and, later, just once a week.

I stand by the door at the beginning of the period, waiting for the class. The teachers were to stand by the entrance to help police the traffic. Today, Friday, the students would be extra rambunctious, so more observing. A student walks up to me and asks me if I heard President Kennedy's news was shot. I said I didn't hear anything. The class comes, and there is no sound from anyone, nothing. I look around, and the guys are just sitting there, quiet. It's Friday, the last day before a weekend, the last period of the day, and these guys are just sitting there. A student said they heard the President had been shot. I said if this is true, we will hear something from the office. Five seconds after I said that Mr. Elmerick announced the President had been shot. It's quiet. I look at these guys, and I see concerned faces.

Five minutes later, the announcement said The President had died. They are looking down and silent; it is quiet, with no sound. I did not mention anything about working on an assignment. Mr. Elmerick said there would be no school on Monday, a National Day of Mourning. Just then, one student jumps up and starts yelling, indicating he is happy there is no school on Monday. We all are startled at this response. Another jumps up and starts yelling at the first guy about the seriousness of what just happened. He approaches the first student with his fists clenched and anger etched on his face. I approach the first student as the angry student hurries to confront the "happy" student. I stand between the two and talk to the angry student, but he is yelling his displeasure. The "happy "student sits down, and we wait until the end of the period. I tell the "happy" student he is not excused. After several minutes, I mentioned that he should go home a different way.

I told the story at the faculty meeting and asked who the boys were. I mentioned their names and heard that I should have taken more time separating the students. That was 1963.

It's 1989; I have been laid off from teaching and working in a machine shop. The man in charge of this department was in that class in 1963. He remembers that confrontation and said he and many other students wish I had taken more time separating the two students.

The student teaching semester ended in late December, and I had one more semester to complete before graduating. Those classes were at night, which allowed me to work and pay some bills. I knew there was a machine shop instructor position at Hower Vocational High School and two Industrial Arts positions at Cuyahoga Falls High School.

Being Hired

Entering KSU in 1959, I was to become an elementary teacher and a coach. It is 1964, graduation is in June, and my name is on the list of graduates. I had two majors, Vocational Education and Industrial Arts. Schools all over were crowded, and teachers were in demand. Cuyahoga Falls School System had two openings in I.A. Mr. Clinton Elmeric, principal at Sill Middle School, recommended me for one position where I did my student teaching. My classes were for the machine shop program. The equipment was three years old and was near what I experienced at Hower as a student. Hower Vocational had an opening, too, and their pay scale was higher than Cuyahoga Falls. I was given credit for two years in the military, which put me at the same level as the Akron pay scale. Joanne and I discussed the best system and decided on the Falls System. Looking back, it was the best for my family and me.

Joanne Working Part-Time

Joanne got pregnant in 1960 and could not work; Dr. Rogers let her go because the substitute lady wanted the job. All hell broke loose with the ladies in the Medical Assistant Group. They came to her rescue and offered help the best they could. The one offer was many would want her to fill in when they were on vacation. After Christine was born, Joanne worked for several doctors and commented on how easy that position was. One doctor told her she should go home before 5:00 pm. Jo had a few things to finish, but the Doctor told her those things could wait for tomorrow. Several Doctors asked her if she could be their substitute because of how she did the job. While working for a surgeon, Joanne had nothing to do but answer the phone. She would compare this routine with working for Dr. Rogers and those hectic-pace-working-late days.

Christine, our first daughter, was born November 18, 1961; her projected birth date was January 3. She weighed 3 pounds 10oz and stayed in the hospital until she weighed five pounds. Christine came home before Christmas. Joanne did not work for several months because she was concerned about Chris being born prematurely. The small dining room was the nursery.

Start The House

We started digging our house's foundation in Tallmadge on our fourth wedding anniversary –June 28, 1962. We obtained a loan from Tallmadge's Mogadore Saving and Loan Branch. The bank manager told us that any bank would loan us the money because we had the land and some cash. The one arrangement was to pay the loan interest until I obtained a job teaching after June 1964.

We saw our house before it was built. We went to the Hartville Lumber Company for ideas for homes. We had a floor plan we liked and wanted to know the approximate cost. We sat with a manager and showed him our picture; he looked at it and laughed. He said this is his house, and do we want to see "your house" already built? We traveled to the brick one-level house and enjoyed seeing what we had on a piece of paper. It was amazing to see an idea come to life in minutes. The floor plan was what we wanted; we could not have a fireplace and an attached garage and wanted a basement. Those house plans became ours with a few changes.

Albert knew a carpenter and son who would rough the house under roof. I contracted for the electric, plumbing, heating, and masonry work (the house was brick) with guidance from the Hartville Lumber Company. July was the beginning of our contract, and there was activity at 508 Southeast Ave. to early May 1963.

I had nothing to do except check on the materials and stay out of the skilled tradesmen's way. It was exciting to see the studs that separated the rooms: how the 28 by 50-foot rectangle is made into rooms and hallways. The electricians' strung wire watched the bricks coming up the outside wall, looked out the installed windows, watched the plumber run lines for the kitchen and bathrooms, and imagined the vanity in the bathroom.

The furnace caused some concern. I contracted Dick Lombardy, who played against me in baseball. Dick had an insulation company but sold us the heating system. He and I reviewed the house plans and the features that affect a home's heating -the type of windows, wall and ceiling insulation, and outside construction. Dick suggests a 100,000 BTU GE cast iron furnace. I approved it because he used numbers to obtain the best furnace size for our house. My Uncle Happy, who worked on the side installing furnaces, became excited because Happy thought the furnace was too small for our home based on his experience. Note – that experience was just a guess-and-answer, with no data. My uncle had a 100,000 BTU furnace; his house was half the size of ours, and he would be overworked during the cold weather. My father-in-law was concerned because he helped a company build house and used a larger capacity furnace. I went with what Mr. Lombardy recommended. Both men shook their heads and walked away. Joanne asked me if I believed in what Dick suggested. When the furnace was in the basement, I wondered if it was too small. It was small! Nope, please put it in the order.

On some days when heat is needed, my uncle stays in the basement checking out the furnace. We found this out after we moved into the house. January and February tested the unit with several below-zero days. My Uncle asked to see our gas bill, and when we compared amounts, there was almost no difference; our house had 1400 square feet, and his house was 900 square feet. He and my father-in-law could not believe that.

Insulation in the ceiling was another problem. Albert worked for a company and placed the bails of insulation in the ceiling. He was planning to do that. The home was ready for the insulation; I called and notified Hartville Company. Albert goes out the next day and doesn't see any bails. He called me and said there were no bails. I called Hartville, and they told me the insulation was blown in the ceiling. That was 1962, and the level in the attic is the same today.

My father-in-law knew a finish carpenter, Elmer, who lived behind the house on Bailey Road. His job was the kitchen cupboards and vanity. Albert and I hung all the doors and trim around the doors. Elmer showed us a lot of tricks to make the job easier. First, I had to pick the ¾-inch plywood for Hartville's door and drawer fronts. My father-in-law got so excited picking out plywood that had just the right wood pattern. We could look at 15 to 20 sheets of maple wood to find 3 or 4 matching patterns. He was right; we didn't want a random design in the kitchen.

I installed the Formica and impressed Elmer when I glued edge strips around round corners. I watched Elmer cut wood, pushing the wood past the cutter from the opposite direction. This is extremely dangerous. In the machine shop, this would be called "climb milling." I did the cupboards in the bathrooms and used this procedure. The advantage of this method is it produces a smooth surface, thus eliminating a lot of sanding, but it is extremely dangerous.

Progress was measured in small steps, and we could see our house becoming livable daily. We would come and see this 28 by 50-foot building becoming our house. After attending church, we visited the building that looked like our house. We talked about each room and its plans. We were in our bedroom and began to speak; one look, one embrace, and passionate kisses led us to initiate our bedroom. There was a concern about visitors, but I locked the doors. I would ask her if we could pretend to use the other bedrooms as our bedrooms on other visits. She would look at me and not say a word. Husbands have to learn that looks can be interpreted as words.

I could not answer when we could move in, but Elmer would try to set a date. One date was after Easter. Joanne was happy to figure out what we had and would need regarding furniture or where we could pick up something a relative would give us. One surprise item needed was coat hangers. We took the couch and kitchen items we had in the basement. We received a couple of 4 and 5-drawer cabinets. We did not need a kitchen table because we had a counter we could eat by, just Joanne, Christine in her highchair, and me.

Moving In

I don't know when we moved in, but it had to be around Easter 1963. We were so happy to wake up and check Christine in her room by herself after the 15 months she was in our room on Bailey Road. It seemed there was an echo as we talked. The first meal was reaching into the refrigerator for a glass of milk, looking out the dining room window, and looking at the 20 apple trees. Our kitchen cupboards had a couple of dishes, cups, and eating utensils; the main bathroom was huge compared to the Bailey Road room. The washer and dryer were on the first floor. It was our dream coming true. We had to watch Christine as she walked around lost in this "huge" house. Our curtains were hand-me-downs and were sufficient. Our T.V. was sitting on a kitchen roll-a-way with wheels and the familiar "rabbit ears." The bedrooms had hardwood floors, but the hallways and living room were plywood waiting for carpet. It was simple but thrilling to be in this house. I know Joanne was happy.

Cathleen

Cathy was born on September 16, 1963. Joanne had no trouble with the delivery, except Cathy came out feet first. I guess they pushed her back and turned her around. (that sounds like I am joking about that). I was student teaching at Sill Middle School, and I was excused to bring Joanne and Cathy home. I did and returned to Sill to plan for the next day. After school, I am with Mr. Watts; everyone hears an announcement over the P.A. system. We hear, "Mr. Sipka, your wife called and wants you to come straight home because we left the baby's 6-pack (Enfamil) in the back seat. I got a lot of kidding about that.

The fall quarter of my last year. I experienced the assassination of President Kennedy on Friday and was shocked like everyone. Joanne was home with Chris and had planned to have a baby shower for Phyllis Falkenstine that Friday night. Was the question? Keep it on, or cancel the shower. Considering the day's event, she kept the shower and had a good turnout. I attended the early Mass on Sunday, and Joanne went to the 11 am Mass. Watching the police move Oswald to another facility; everyone saw Ruby step out and shoot Oswald before millions of people. That's a vision I can't forget.

The Early Years

The time is 1963, and we are in the house. During those early days, Joanne became pregnant with Cathy. The first few weeks, Joanne needed help because of morning sickness, and we were concerned that she would have an early delivery like Christine. Joanne's mom helped until Jo could do the usual things by herself. Julia was a God-sent for all her help. I was a half-time student and worked at Main Mold doing all I could. Uncle Happy helped with the yard work, and Aunt Helen would come over and help Joanne in the house. Those days were full of activities, and looking back, I realize how great they were in developing our family into what it is today. Our income was minable, and expenses were common. We didn't miss a meal, and no one complained about our daily lives. Family and friends were donating items to fill our rooms. I remember someone gave us their old curtain for our large living room window; we could now take down the bedsheet. I don't think we hung any pictures yet. We kept thinking about what was to come. I am a fourth-year student taking night classes in Vocational Education.

One story Joanne always mentions is about Aunt Helen's cat. During the summer, Jo would hang clothes to dry on a carousel-type clothesline. She is outside and sees the cat walking up to her, but she pays no attention. The cat rubs against her leg, and when Jo looks down, and sees a snake, she screams and runs away. She does return, but after serious checking.

Third-Year at KSU

September 1962 was the start of the third year at Kent. The classes were in the IA during the day and VE at night. I would work as many hours as I could. It was that daily routine day after day for the fall, then winter, and spring quarters. My grade average was increasing. I made birth announcements in blue and pink designs in the graphics class. We still have a few blue ones somewhere. I made our bedroom furniture in Woods II: a headboard, two nightstands, and a wastepaper basket. I made drawings for a triple dresser and dresser for me but had to wait until Wood III. All the bedroom furniture was walnut wood, and we still use the set.

Our bedroom furniture has a glass top on the two dressers and two end tables because of an accident. We were in the house for a year, and I bought a riding mower because I had to mow our yard and Uncle Happy's yard. I am cutting the front yard; Joanne and the kids are watching me. The blade on the mower propelled a rock and struck our large picture window low on one corner, cracking the glass. The window had to be replaced. The double-pane window is one-fourth of an inch thick. I asked the window company if they could cut pieces to cover the two dressers and end tables.

In the required Machine Shop II class, the instructor asked me to assist him with the basic Machine Shop I class. I also made a classroom presentation, demonstrated some machine procedures, and had to write a paper, and enjoyed teaching.

Senior Year at Kent State

In my senior year at Kent, I was in VoEd and Ind Arts and worked 30 + hours at Main Mold and Machine, and we are in the house at Southeast Ave. in Tallmadge. Joanne was sick with morning sickness and had help from her mother. Reflecting on that time of our life was the most exciting. I know Joanne was happy, as was I. Every day was an adventure leading to our future; what kind of future? The new big house with white walls and plywood floor in the living room; the big back yard with deers and pheasants; hand-me-down curtains and kitchen utensils that didn't match. The back porch was extra concrete blocks with no side rails, no grass to mow, and piles of dirt to spread. It was a pleasure to enter the house, look around, and think we had a castle. We had to look for Christine because she could be in any of those rooms. We sat on the hand-me-down couch, told each other how good we felt, and talked about what might happen. I know we used to talk about that first kiss and imagine if I didn't kiss her or if she would have got mad at me. I made enough money to pay our bills, and we didn't miss any meals.

Jaycees

We wanted to meet other young families in Tallmadge. I joined the Tallmadge Jaycees in 1963, an organization of men up to 35. I joined and was anxious to become involved, but my involvement was limited because of school and work. Joanne is pregnant and due in September.

Our walls were plastered and white, and we were told to wait until the plaster dries out. I believe the time was to wait one year. Joanne mentioned that the white walls were getting to her. We were to wait. I helped with a Jaycee project at Christmas time, during which the Jaycee men would deliver baskets of food and gifts to needed families in Tallmadge. We went to seven or eight homes, and I saw bad situations and the rooms' conditions, walls, and floors. One house didn't have electric lights. I returned home and told Joanne what I saw and that the white walls were beautiful. The plywood floor in the living room was also lovely. We talked about how lucky we were and our better days were ahead.

We became active with Joanne, helping other wives in the Saturday morning three-hour daycare center for `disabled children (held in the small Tallmadge library). The purpose was to allow the mothers of these children to have three hours for themselves. She would return, talking about what she experienced and how good she felt. Joanne was there every Saturday; the center was open, and she met many wives. I could see her feelings for people, especially handicapped children.

We were members of the Jaycees until I reached the age of 35. We joined when we were 25 years old and had ten pleasurable years. We enjoyed the parties and yearly installation dinners. I recommend every young married couple join an organization because you meet people your age. I remained a member but not a voting member and was also called an "Exhausted Rooster." We both enjoyed the years in the Jaycees.

The Ten Years That Made Us A Family 1963 – 1973

The time was 1963 to 1973, and I had tears in my eyes when I thought about those days. What will tomorrow bring? We could only pay the interest on our house loan and looked in the paper for sales. When should I start leveling the dirt around the yard? Uncle Happy said he would have the guy plow more of our yard to plant a garden. We caned food we grew and never missed a meal. I learned how to take care of our apple trees to have bug-free apples and mix the ingredients for spraying our trees. We planted flowers and shrubs around the house. We obtained a dog and built a fence to handle the dog (and girls). The girls start school, and Joanne becomes involved with the David Bacon School. Should we have a turn-a-round in our front yard? Backing out on Southeast Ave would be too dangerous. You could see Joanne and me loving this growth of our family and home.

I started my Master's program in 1970 during the summer. The class was for Vocational teachers from all disciplines. I met a man who was an air-conditioning instructor in Cleveland, and he arranged to install a full-house air-conditioning system on the weekend. We had a lot of company during the hot summer days and didn't mind.

The Trouble With Mortgage Payments

Our house started the week in June 1963. We arranged for the Mogadore Saving and Loan Company to handle the load. Our money was used first; after that, money came from the loan. In setting up the loan, we asked for a special condition. I expected to obtain a teaching job in September of 1964 and asked if we would be allowed to pay just the interest each month until receiving the pay from teaching. Mr. Eicherberry, the bank president, agreed. The monthly payment was $90 with $60 interest and a $30 principal. I would go to the bank, present my loan book, pay the $60, and leave. Early in 1964, The First National Bank bought the Mogadore Bank. We received an IBM card from the First National Bank for the same amounts. I still pay the $60. After a couple of months, we received a letter from First National asking why I paid just $60. I went to the bank and showed the letter to Mr. Eicherberry. He proceeded to call someone and explain that the Mogadore Bank was a Country Bank, and that's how country banks do business, and this arrangement would end in October. Here's an old country banker telling an IBM banker how banking was done before. The IBM card changed for a few months until the October payment.

Carol

Carol was born on September 13, 1965, and I was entering my second year teaching. Joanne was busy with Christine, age four, Cathy, age two, and a new baby. She had her hands full. I thought she was happy even with all this responsibility. We were adding pieces of furniture and had the walls painted. I had just worked the summer break at Ferriot Brothers shop, and the added income helped. We were in the Jaycees and made new friends from young families. Looking back, it was a happy and hectic time. One thing that happened was Cathy, age two, fell down the basement steps. She was taken to the Doctor, and there were no injuries. Joanne felt bad, but we all made her feel it was OK. Her dad came and helped put a chain lock device on the basement door. Joanne was 100% mother to those three girls; She loved the work.

Uncle Happy

Frank Starr was a different individual who was liked by some but not enjoyed by others. He had a course demean. Starr was not his real last name; it was Giviazda, a good old Polish name. I know how to spell the last name because I have Uncle Happy and Aunt Helen's wedding certificate. Happy was Aunt Helen's (Uncle Johnny's wife) uncle. Helen's mother and Happy were brother and sister. I hope that doesn't get you confused. I had three Helens in my family – my mom, Uncle Johnny's Helen, and Uncle Happy's Helen (my dad's sister and aunt). Wait, I should include my sister Helene; That should make four.

Happy and Helen had no children. They were close to my mom and dad and spent time playing cards once a month. He gave my sisters and me gifts on different occasions. For example, Happy saw my sister going on a date all dressed up, and he bought her some nice presents the next time they visited.

Aunt Helen

Uncle Happy died in 1967. Aunt Helen was able to drive and stay in her house. I remember Chris and Cathy would visit her daily as good neighbors. We often had her over for supper, and she liked the visits, too. There were times we all would go to picnics with a family that we hadn't met but were cousins of Aunt Helen. I remember two trips to Port Clinton, Ohio, for an all-day picnic. Aunt Helen enjoyed those times. Unfortunately, she became ill with stomach problems and lived with us in Christine's bedroom. During the day, Helen had a few visitors (Chris, Cathy, and Carol). The girls would hold Helen's hand and sit with her, which helped her feel welcome.

We talked about these things years before when Uncle Happy offered the lot. We agreed to take care of Aunt Helen after Uncle Happy's death. Joanne, her parents, my parents, and I talked about what we would commit to doing for Aunt Helen a few times. What would it be like years later, and for how long? How severe would her condition be? I remember the look on Joanne's face when she wanted me to say "yes" because it would give us a house. There was a look on Joanne's face when she was told she couldn't continue in the nursing program because she failed chemistry. She oversees the whole hospital ward, with a sick patient in the middle bedroom. Her job now as a nurse was 24 hours, seven days a week. Those hours working for Dr. Rogers and other doctors involving sick people were her calling. She performed this calling in different ways. Sister Benilda, Helen's sister, was allowed to come and help for many days. Sister wanted Helen to go to a hospital in Michigan to try a new procedure to treat cancer, but Aunt Helen said no. Sister was sure Helen received all the final church rites. Aunt Helen died in our home with someone with her. We both stood there and said we lived up to our agreement with Uncle Happy. That was Joanne at her best – taking care of people.

Life With The Family at 508 Southeast Ave.

Our above-ground pool was enjoyed by all of us

Chris and Cathy (note the temporary back porch)

When you hear "Our above-ground pool." (*I would guess the year is 1966*) One can visualize a large pool, but our pool was small, and it accommodated most of us. Joanne was not working outside the home but working full-time with the three girls. I always believed staying home with the children was a job, and that's why I worked during the summer months to add to our income. We didn't have a garage and had one car. Mr. Haskal Jones, our neighbor, helped us with a large garden. We grew and canned vegetables and then purchased a freezer. Our apple trees were cared for, and we had apples to sell and use for cider. During the fall, I would have bags of apples in the van and sell them to teachers. I also gave apples to students; they kidded me about the teacher giving students apples instead of the other way.

Our backyard became a playground

Joanne and her mom took the girls to this attraction in Pennsylvania while
I was in graduate school. The big deal was a goat ate Cathy's tag on her
top, which I heard about in emotional detail when they got home.

Joanne is preparing for a bridal shower.

Joanne was busy with the girls when they were not old enough to attend school. She took pride in the way the girls were dressed and looked. The sewing machine was kept alive with matching outfits. We began to furnish our house instead of those hand-me-downs from others. We purchased our carpet for the living room and dining set, the sofa, and the recliner. We added a cardboard fireplace for the Christmas holidays so we could hang our Christmas stockings. Of course, the TV was up to date.

I fixed the basement so our girls and visitors could play there. We had two tricycles and a push pedal car, and all would circle the cellar at an unsafe speed on a 20 by 35-foot oval. This activity wasn't just from our three but six other cousins the same age. Christine was my parents' first grandchild, but three more kids were born within two months. Then, there were three more cousins within the next year. My cousin, Jack, had a boy and a girl; sometimes, we had six to eight kids close to the same age, none old enough to go to school. Our main worry was the kids going up and down the stairs. I had to enclose the sides of the stairs because we didn't want anyone falling off the side of the stairs. Our old couch was now downstairs, plus other chairs. We had a lot of birthday parties there, and we saved our new furniture upstairs.

I built shelves on the end of the basement for storage. We canned a lot and bought and stored canned goods on sale. Joanne and I would hide the Christmas presents and nail the one corner door shut. Years later, they told us they knew how to open the door, check out the presents, and nail the door shut.

My daughter Carol reminded me that I made space for a library when I built shelves. I was friends with the man in charge of the school warehouse because we stored some program supplies there. There would be discarded books, and I could bring different books home and place them in our "Library." The girls played "Library," and each girl would drive the push pedal car to the library and check out a book. There are still some old 1967-type books there that are ready for the great-grandkids. I found a copy of "The Dragon Seed" by Pearl S. Buck, a classic, and "Two Boys a Tree." by Gates Huber Salesbury. There are many others there for the great-grandkids. The thought is, will those in the future read books?

We had a live Christmas tree for many years, and the girls would decorate the tree. My job was to stand it up and place the angel on top. I was in the Jaycees, and they would sell trees, and I would buy a tree with a crooked base at a reduced price. I would have to improvise to make it look straight. Joanne told me one time to hang it from the ceiling.

I fixed most of one side of the basement and put it into a rec. room, and that started more activity downstairs. I believe the first big event we were to have was Cathy's surprise 16th birthday party on Saturday, September 17, 1979. We just installed the carpet. Hurricane "Fredrick" came up from the Gulf of Mexico Thursday evening; No Big Deal! Friday morning, I got a call from my neighbor, who wanted to know if we had water in our basement. I looked, and we did – up to the first step. I called the school and told them we had a problem with water in the basement, and I was excused. I drove to a rental place and rented the last water pump. We set the pump up and were careful because we had a dehumidifier plugged in and had to be cautious. Cathy's birthday party was canceled. We carried the 13 by 26-foot carpet outside, placed it in the front yard to dry, and kept it there until the next day. It was rainwater and not sewer water. We scrubbed the basement and carpet and put it back.

We would have the Sipka Family over for Christmas gatherings. Have a good time. Another year, we held a party for the Cuyahoga Falls Vocational Staff because Mr. Anderson had a problem at his house and could not have it.

Joanne and I would try to discuss things with the girls and ask for their opinions. I attended Kent State's summer programs and had a classmate who taught heating and air-conditioning in Cleveland. (*I will say it is the summer of 1972*). He said he could install a unit, but I would have to pick up the parts in Cleveland. We asked the girls which they would like: A) an above-ground pool or B) whole-house air-conditioning. The vote was three for a pool (the three girls) to two (Jo and me). One of us said that because we would use our money, we each would have two votes; thus, the total vote would be four for air conditioning and three for pool. There were a lot of comments, but we looked at each other and smiled. The air-conditioning system was installed, and after a few days of comfort in the house, the girls commented the air-conditioning was a better idea. We invited Joanne's parents over as often as they wanted.

From 1964, when we moved in, to the beginning of the girls going to school (1967), it was a period of full-time work for Joanne as a mother and wife. I believe she loved it and felt happy. I felt like a father and was delighted.

Girls Going To School – David Bacon

Our three daughters were two years apart; the days turned to weeks and then years. Christine, who started in 1967, catches the school bus to David Bacon Elementary Grade School, and Joanne had those feelings; a mother has seen a child leaving home. And every two years, another girl starts the education process. Joanne is now involved with grade school activities with different teachers. She was a roommother for each of the girls and would volunteer to help with classes. I know she enjoyed this involvement. Next comes the Middle School and then the High School.

81

Tallmadge Middle School and The High School

The three grown Sipka girls are keeping us busy

The girls advanced to middle school and high school. The experience at the High School was exciting because of the skills the girls acquired from swim classes at the YMCA.

We enrolled Christine in swim lessons at the Tallmadge YMCA to learn the basic skills, and the instructor recommended we enroll her in the Cuyahoga Falls AAU swim team. The summer season was over, so we enrolled her as a ten-year-old on the Cuyahoga Falls YMCA swim team. She enjoyed the season, and now we have Cathy taking swim lessons. As a ten-year-old, she followed the same path as Chris to the AAU summer team. Lastly, Carol followed the same path as her sisters and was on the summer AAU team.

Our family had the three girls swimming during the winter months for the YMCA and the summers for the Water Works AAU team. We traveled to many cities in Ohio and surrounding states for swim meets. The girls advanced in their abilities to master the skills needed to win their events. It was the thrill of victory for our family.

Chris enters the high school (NOTE – Tallmadge High School was a three-year high school.) In 1978, The State of Ohio started varsity swimming for girls. Chris was in the 11th grade and swam in the first girls' swim meet. As a 10th grader, Cathy was in high school the next year and swam and advanced from the district swim meet to the Ohio State Swimming Championship held at The Ohio State Pool in Columbus.

The Tallmadge YMCA joined the leagues of YMCAs that had swimming teams. We had a five-lane – 25-yard pool. The boys' and girls' teams were competitive because of the coaches and girls who started swimming in grade school. Joanne and I were active in running the meets. I was a starter, and Joanne worked the scoring table.

In 1981, seven girls entered the 10th grade, and the idea was to have a high school varsity swim team. School officials refused to allow a varsity team. Still, they allowed ten girls to compete in 3 varsity meets against other varsity teams to qualify as a team to score team points in the district and state championship meets. The girls lost the three swim meets but placed fourth in the district and eighth at the Ohio State Girls Swimming Championships. As a tenth grader, Carol placed third in the 500-yard freestyle event and scored points in the 100-yard butterfly event. Cathy placed in her two events; the 400-yard free relay placed eighth, and all added points. We reported this accomplishment to the Tallmadge Board of Education. One board member asked how many teams were there? We mentioned 67. He thought nine teams.

The next year the team had three meets but won the last meet. At District, we were 15[th,] and at The Ohio Girls Swimming Championships, the team placed 15th. Again, Cathy and Carol and the 400-yard free relay scored points.

That was the last year Tallmadge High School had a swim team until later in 2005.

YMCA

Belly Dancing

We used the Tallmadge YMCA for the girls for swim lessons. Cathy took ballet classes and performed in the group's year-end shows; the families would come and sit around the hall and watch the dancers. Unfortunately, she became involved with the Y's swim team and couldn't continue her dance classes. Joanne signed up for a class called Belly Dancing and got a lot of kidding from me. I said I would like to watch the ladies learn the routines. I watched Cathy; why can't I watch the ladies? When and where will the end of the class recital be? I am sure the other husbands would like to see the new skills the wives learned. She heard my question, "Have you learned how to move the tassels in circles?" She would shake her head and give me that look. Jo did have some new moves; the class was worth the money. Was there an advanced class? "No," was the reply.

YMCA and Swimming AAU

The Tallmadge YMCA offered swim lessons, and Chris was the first to participate. She learned fast, and the instructor recommended Chris join the Cuyahoga Falls YMCA swim team. So she did, and our family enjoyed the numerous swim meets at different YMCA facilities. Chris swam for the Water Works AAU swim team; we traveled to various cities for multi-day meets. Cathy, eight years old, and Carol, six, took lessons at the YMCA. Cathy joined the Falls YMCA team as a nine-year-old. Carol was still at the YMCA. All three girls could test out of the Y's different categories and became "Sharks." They could perform all the requirements to become lifeguards but were too young.

In 1972, all three girls were on the Water Works Team - Chris (11 years old), Cathy (9 years old), and Carol (7 years old). They could all win trophies, medals, and ribbons during the summer. I made up a bulletin board displaying all the awards, filling it up quickly.

The girls grew and advanced in their swimming skills from swimming in the summer and winter seasons. Jo and I didn't complain about our involvement. Our desire to help, helped them to improve. We had a van and took other swimmers to meets because their parents couldn't attend. Our girls and their friends enjoyed the trips. Our van had bench seats, and we could have as many as six other girls with Jo and me. It was "Stan and his green van!". One daughter said that one girl mentioned that she (my daughter) was lucky to have parents interested in their kids. We did miss some family gatherings because we were out of town at swim meets. We ensured we were not "little league parents" who would yell at the kids if they didn't win. One parent mentioned it was too bad that I didn't have a boy to play baseball because he knew I loved baseball and had success playing it. I told him the girls gave me enough satisfaction not to miss baseball. Both of us were thrilled at what swimming did for our family. Instead of bats and baseball gloves, we talked "Speedo" suits, goggles, and caps. I made a special "machine" and bench that allowed the girls to simulate the swim strokes in our basement during school and the fall and winter YMCA seasons. The improvement was amazing. The weights were very light, and I found an old clock with a second hand. The girls could practice all four strokes, using the last time they swam that event on the machine. We never yelled or told them to go downstairs and practice. We were more interested in their school activities.

The girls were Christine, 14, Cathy, 12, and Carol, 10, and we tried a different summer swim team. The team's home pool was a lake. All the meets were away meets. Carol, at this time, was one of the best ten and under girls; she could swim and win in all four strokes (her backstroke wasn't her best). At the meet, the coaches meet and go over the events. Our coach knew Carol's skills, and when asking about the other team's ten-year-old girls, most team managers said they didn't have any ten and under girls. So our coach would say," To save time, we will let our one girl swim against the other teams' boys. Invariably, the other coach would say, "Do you think that's fair to the girl?" Our coach would say he's OKAY with that. In the six or seven meets, Carol, swimming the four strokes, never lost. I would watch Carol swim the 25 yards, get out of the pool, grab her towel as the other team swimmer touches the wall, and look to see where that girl is; she is out of the pool.

Joanne Will Drink A Beer

The year was 1972, and we bought a Volkswagen van, our first van for traveling to meets. The three-day meet was in Huntington, West Virginia. The difference with this meet was it was on Thursday, Friday, and Saturday, not Sunday. The city had the Blue Rule, which meant no activity on Sunday. Our five, Mrs. Blair and her daughter, Sherry, traveled there. We arrived, checked in at the hotel, and went to a restaurant. We came back to the motel. I applied the brakes, we stopped, and then the brake pedal went to the floor. I tried the brake pedal again, and it would go to the floor – NO BRAKES. I didn't say anything to Joanne. I checked under the car and saw the fluid on the ground – NO BRAKES. I still didn't say anything.

> NOTE: *I attended summer school at Kent State in the graduate program and the two classes I had required no absence. If absent, I would be dropped from the courses with no credit. I had to get back on Monday.*

I talked with the other fathers, who agreed to help drive our kids and Sherry to the meet. It's Thursday, and a Volkswagen dealer was next door to the motel -WHAT LUCK. Early Friday, I carefully drove the van to the dealer. Yes, it's a bad brake cylinder. I am happy now because I will be back in time for Monday's classes. Late Friday, the company told me the replacement cylinder would arrive next Monday; they didn't have one in stock. Joanne and I did a lot of thinking. I had to return to the classes. Flying was not possible; renting a car was possible. I offered Plan "A" to the dealer. Since the cylinder has two sections -front brakes and rear brakes, and the front brakes are not working, pinch off the front brakes and depend on the back brakes. Everyone in that garage yelled, "NO," which is unsafe, and they won't do that. The next day is Sunday, and if I leave early in the morning on the East-West interstate, I could be in Ohio by noon, and there would be another 120 miles to our house. Absolutely "NO" was their reply; It's too dangerous. I agreed to sign a paper acknowledging I would not hold them responsible after hearing all the danger with my request. One mechanic gave me his telephone number and asked if I would call him when we got home. I told him I would call. Joanne insisted on going with me because she could help watch behind and for other problems. The other parents took our kids and Mrs. Blair and Sherry home. Early Sunday morning, we slowly drove to the gas station and got a full tank of gas; Joanne went inside and bought snacks and drinks to keep from stopping. It's a little after six AM, and we are off. We drove East, traveling at the 65-mile speed limit, watching behind. The Sunday morning traffic was light. We arrived at Routes 88 and

77 intersection around noon and had no problems. Joanne kept massaging my neck and watching behind. I made sure I had plenty of room in the front. I felt we had one good stop with the rear brakes and hoped we didn't need it. I don't remember if Joanne drove, but our concentration was so intense we didn't think we were tired. We notice the gas gauge and believe we can't make it home without stopping for gas. We stopped at a gas station by the Football Hall of Fame. I carefully slowed down, timed the traffic light, turned right left into the station, and coasted to a stop. It was potty time for snacks and drinks. We slowly pulled out, timing the one light and back on 77. We began to relax but still were looking in all directions. We are at the central interchange and a few miles from Rt. 532 -Southeast Ave – home of Joanne, the girls, and Stan. We remember to start to slow down as we approach Southeast Ave. We are on SE and almost see our house, which is just two miles away. The light at the six corners is green, and we can smell our place. We come over a hill and see our house, but there is a long line of cars traveling in the other direction; I begin to downshift to turn in our driveway slowly because we can end up in our backyard. Finally, it's time to turn. I look in the mirror, and here comes a guy speeding around the four cars behind me; I hit the brakes, and we stop. The turn and downshifting to a slow pace to our backyard. We sit there and take a deep breath. I announce I will drink a beer! Joanne says I will drink a beer too. We did embrace and comment on how crazy we were. I told her I was glad she came with me. She said I would not let you go by yourself. I know the word LOVE was mentioned.

I called the dealership guy and told him we arrived safely. He said I worried him and thanked me for calling. Our kids arrived much later than us.

Swimming After High School

Our swimming interest continued when Cathy, first and then Carol, went to Youngstown State University. Joanne and I watched Cathy's first swim meet at YSU, and the freshman girl swimmers broke every record. Coach Joe Kemper recruited seven girls who produced a new pool record for every event that first meet. We attended the NCCA Division II Championship at Hofstra University in Hempstead, Long Island, New York.

Carol went to YSU the next year, and the team became stronger with several new freshmen swimmers. We got to fly to Fort Lauderdale, Florida, for the NCCA Division II Championships. Besides watching the swim meet, we were there during the college spring break. Jo and I saw some interesting activities. We couldn't imagine how ten girls could fit in one room; the tub was used as a bed.

We flew to these events and had a hard time during the flight, but the hostess helped us with several bags.

The family after college and competitive swimming

<u>Swimming Even Today</u>

Even today, the time, money, and effort we put into the girls' swimming have paid off. Cathy's two boys swam and also played football. It was a sight to see Corey, a linebacker, swimming and winning the freestyle events. The same happened with Nicholas, who also wrestled and threw the shot put and discus. Cathy manages the pool and aquatic programs at Akron General Medical program. Corey is the swim coach at Kent Roosevelt High School and has recently been appointed Kent Pool director. Cathy was inducted into the YSU Sports Hall of Fame.

Carol is a swimming official who participates in pool activities as a Kent Roosevelt High School teacher. She teaches swimming to students as part of the physical education program at Kent. Monica, Joey, Julia, and Mellisa, Carol's four children, swam in high school and did well. Monica swam at YSU and later at Mount Union College. Julia swam in two district championships.

Joanne and I spent much time helping the girls and grandkids with their activities and enjoyed watching their efforts. We would come tired and proud whether they won or didn't win. One day during the YMCA season, a daughter told us that a girl we would take to meets in our van commented how lucky we (the girls) were to have parents interested in their kids. That was our reward.

We Purchase A New Van For Our Trip

I continued my graduate courses and obtained my Master's degree in 1972. I mentioned that I owe everything to Joanne for helping me achieve my goals. I wanted her to go on that stage dressed in the cap and gown and accept the diploma. After receiving the diploma, I looked up and saw Joanne and the girls. Then, I waved and threw a kiss. After writing this paragraph, I relived that time and day. Thank you, Joanne; I love you.

We never took a long vacation because I would work during the summer and be involved with swimming. Jo and I decided we would take three weeks to go to California to visit my sister. That was to be a present for all of us.

We ordered a new Chevy van, which is scheduled to arrive in May. We are buying clothes and obtaining maps to prepare for the four days of driving the 2400 miles. We got a phone call from the dealer asking us to come to the dealership. It was good; our van has arrived!!! "NO," the van can't be delivered for some reason – SORRY! That was what we heard. Now What??? We had two weeks to figure out how and what to do. We thought of canceling the trip. The girls were upset; well, we all were.

I was leaving school and decided to drive home differently and pass the many dealerships on Front Street. I notice a green Ford van and stop. It's a well-equipped van with low mileage. It was a stick shift, but we both drove stick shift cars. I drove it home, and you should see the excitement when we all came in and sat on the seats. I heard, "BUY IT!" We had a van, and the trip was on.

I fixed the van so we could sleep inside. I removed the last bench seat and placed a plywood sheet on top of the wheel wells; thus, we had space to hold our suitcases like the trunk of a car. Two baby mattresses were placed on top of this plywood; two girls could sleep there. I built an upper bed for Chris. Joanne had the bench seat, and I slept on the floor. Our first stop was at my sister Rita's house in Indianapolis for one night. Rita's three kids and ours had a good time. We slept in their house.

The next stop would be the Maramack Caverns west of St. Louis, where we would sleep in the van for the first time. We toured the caverns and prepared for bed; Joanne and the girls went to the shelter, washed, and returned. I grabbed my towel and bag and walked to the shelter. I looked up to locate the men's entrance and had to walk around to the other side. I saw the MEN's sign and walked in. I heard a shower running and looked down at a pile of clothes – THEY WERE WOMEN'S CLOTHES. I backed up and looked at the sign "MEN." I walked in and heard the lady tell me this was the lady's side. I replied, "No." this was the men's side, and she had the wrong side. I walked to the other half of the men's section and wondered if I could have been in trouble if this lady had started screaming about me being in the "wrong restroom."

We go to sleep, and I can't sleep squeezed between the front and bench seats. I toss and turn and feel claustrophobic. I was almost going to go out and sleep on a picnic table. But I stayed in and didn't sleep well or at all. Traveling to the next stop, we would sleep in a Holiday Inn.

We planned to stop at Albuquerque, New Mexico, but decided to stop earlier because the weather looked bad. Fortunately for us, Albuquerque had tornadoes and experienced a lot of damage.

We stopped at the corner of the four states, and we each placed a hand and foot in a different State. It's Arizona, Utah, New Mexico, and Colorado. We were surprised how little was around this site, with no stores, motels, or restaurants.

We planned to stay a day in Flagstaff, Arizona, because Diana's mother and father-in-law lived there. The day we left Tallmadge, Joanne's parents and sister's family left town, too. We thought we might meet in Flagstaff. They took the northern route, and we took the southern route. We arrived at Mr. Fred Kempton's house and had no idea where Joanne's parents were (remember, no cell phones). We checked in at the hotel, called Mr Kempton, and gave him our room telephone number. Diana called five minutes later and said they had just arrived. We settled in and drove back to the Kempton and spent time there. Mr. Kempton took all of us out for dinner.

We all went to a Mexican Restaurant, and I sat opposite Mrs. Kempton. She was a thin, quiet, petite lady. I asked what would be a good dinner to order because I had no experience eating Mexican food. A meal was ordered, and when it arrived, I watched others and what sauces they would place on the food. I noticed Mrs. Kempton doused her meal with a bottle, and I thought to do the same. I was told to taste a little from that bottle because that was the hottest liquid on the table. I placed a little on my tongue and quickly drank some water. For her, it was like me putting ketchup on a hotdog. She smiled and said it didn't bother her.

LAS VEGAS

During our conversation, someone mentioned Las Vegas and its proximity to Flagstaff. It was Saturday, and Joanne, her parents, and I decided to go to Vegas on Sunday and spend the day and return on Monday. We arrived in Vegas, checked in with two rooms, and visited the sites. Joanne and I were eager to put money in the slot machines, but Albert kept talking about wasting one's money and how the machines are set to keep people from winning. We would look at each other, and you could see our disappointment, but we didn't play the slots. We saw a show where the chorus line of ladies was topless, and we were ten feet from the stage. We were close to our motel, walked back, said goodnight to her parents, and returned to the Casino. We played the slots until two in the morning, returned to the room, and slept a few hours. Jo's parents didn't know we went back. We told each other we were a couple of teenagers sneaking out on a date. We won some coins and placed them in a compartment so Albert wouldn't see them. I remember how we commented on how dirty our hands were from handling the coins. We enjoyed the return trip to Flagstaff on Monday. On Tuesday, we returned to Kempton's house to say goodbye, and Mr. Kempton placed a plastic water bag on our car's bumper. Mr. Kempton said we were driving through the desert, and extra water is like a spare tire. It's important to have it, and hope you don't need it. So, California, here we come!!!

We left early in the morning to avoid the sun mid-day, and arriving in Stockton was a pleasant sight. We went from nothing but sand to wall-to-wall houses in four hours.

Our three girls had fun at Arlene's house with – Laurie, Bryon, and Mark. Uncle Don worked at a bank. We would spend a day at home enjoying her backyard pool and go somewhere the next day. Knott's Berry Farm, Tijuana, Mexico, Disney World, and San Diego Zoo were there.

SAN DIEGO ZOO

We arrived at the zoo and promptly set up the procedure if someone got lost. The person lost should walk back to a statue of a Gorilla at the entrance and wait. All the kids agreed to those instructions. The eight of us began the walk, and I enjoyed the zoo.

We are looking at the monkey area and are being entertained by the animals. I look around, and all the family is out of sight! This area was at an intersection of three paths to other parts of the zoo. What path should I take? I stayed there thinking they would return, and no one returned. Let's see the instructions stated that if lost, return to the statute. I did return but took my time and observed one path by myself. (can you keep a secret? I enjoyed the walk by myself). I sit on a bench by the statue; the family returns after an hour or two. That was the main topic of conversation for a long time. Even now, a daughter will mention I got lost at the zoo.

Uncle Don took a day off, and we all took a boat trip to Santa Catalina Island. It was a large vessel with multiple decks. We were excited to be on the ocean until Joanne and I got seasick. Jo had it worse than me, but I didn't want to move from my chair near the railing. The kids were having a ball, running around like they were on land. Both of us sat a lot when we arrived on the island. I remember watching the ship moving out of the enclosed area with a smooth ocean and then noticing the choppy water. It's too late to change our minds. The ride back wasn't as bad.

We spent the Fourth of July at the ocean and were anxious to watch the fireworks display from a pier. We are sitting there, and it seems that everyone has some fireworks. Rockets were flying everywhere. It was scary sitting there watching out for rockets. It was like a war zone. We decided to move away from the beach because of the danger.

SWIM TEAM OF PLACENCIA - S.T.O.P.

Our girls had been swimming with the WaterWorks AAU team and took time off when we went to California. My sister told a neighbor that her nieces swam in Tallmadge and could practice a few times to keep in shape. "Sure," was the reply. The girls did and made an impression on the coaching staff. We were asked if they could swim at the next meet, but they had to become members. The meet was against Mission Viejo, the team that had not lost a meet. This team has swimmers that have won medals at the Olympics. The head coach was Mark Schubert, who coached at Water Works a few years ago and knew our girls. The swim team of Placencia (S.T.O.P) wore red suits, and our girls had black suits. Cathy and Carol scored individual points and helped in the relays, and STOP beat Mission by that amount. Joanne and I had people wanting to help find a house to buy in Placencia.

The year is 1984, and Cathy is visiting Ohio State University regarding a swimming scholarship. She met the head coach and was introduced to the assistant coaches. A lady coach mentioned she coached at Mission Vie, and Cathy said she swam against the mission a couple of years ago. The lady stops and yells, "You and your sister were wearing black suits." Cathy answered, "Yes," the coach said they wondered where the two of you lived.

We returned to the northern route, which took us past Reno, Nevada. The kids put their feet in Lake Tahoe, and we played the slot machines. This time, Joanne won a jackpot. I was going to take a picture but was stopped and told it was against the law.

SALT LAKE CITY, UTAH – MORMAN TABERNACLE

We stopped In Salt Lake City, Utah, toured the Morman Tabernacle, and heard the famous choirs sing. The buildings were interesting, but hearing the chorus was a highlight for me. A strange thing happened in the parking lot. I notice a van with Ohio Plates and recognize Bob Gruber's van; he teaches with me in the machine trades program. He and his family are in Utah visiting the site also. I don't have time to find him and talk, but I mentioned this when I saw him in school.

We traveled alongside fast-moving rapids in Colorado and watched guys battling the water. The girls were watching, and suddenly, they turned and yelled, "THEY JUST MOONED US!" I complained that Jo or one of the girls would yell, "Look at this or that." I wanted to look too but didn't know which way to turn – left or right? I told them to say, "Look at that (??) on the right or left." The roads in the Rockies are two lanes and full of curves as you travel around the mountains; thus, the driver must be alert to driving and have no distractions. The girls enjoyed the scenery in the mountains, but next came the flat land of Nebraska, Montana, and Iowa, Illinois, which was boring. Did we hear how many miles to go? A few times. They learned to read road maps. They were good, and we felt the trip was a success.

Our life returned to normal: girls in school, Joanne at home, and my teaching. Joanne took on a part-time at Tallmadge Middle School as a lunchroom monitor and then a detention monitor. She started working more with the schools, and we discussed her working enough to help with a retirement plan. Her goal would be 20 years.

The second trip to California happened in 1977. I know that because Chris was going to drive when possible. The girls are now Chris, 16, Cathy, 14, and Carol, 12. They remembered the long, boring time in the car and had a plan: They asked if they could fly to Denver, Colorado, and we would pick them up instead of riding with them. We countered with our plan: WE WOULD fly to Denver, and THEY WOULD meet us in Dever, Colorado. Both plans were rejected.

The girls were in High School, and these long trips would not happen because each girl would go in a different direction. So it would be Joanne and me now.

No More Vans!

We plan on buying another car, and Joanne tells me, "NO MORE VANS!" I get the message. We walk with a salesperson, me in front and Jo behind, looking at the dealership's sedans. Joanne yells for me to look at what she found: a VAN. I looked at the salesperson and said she had told me, "Don't even look at a van!" What is she sitting in? It is a well-equipped van with captain chairs and a fancy interior. When I asked her why, she told me to forget she didn't want a van; now she wants a van. She liked the fancy interior; we bought it and enjoyed it for a long time.

In 2012, we both wanted a new car for Joanne and not a used one. I suggested we both go and look because it's her car. She wanted a new Chevrolet and told me to pick a new car. I bring home a royal blue basic vehicle; no, it has to be red. I returned and requested a red car, but the basic Chevrolet doesn't come in red. So we bought a red Malibu, which cost a lot, but Joanne was happy. She commented that it was the first car she owned.

Trips To Italy (1973)

Joanne went to Italy twice, once with her father, mother, sister, Diane, Ed (Diana's husband), and Eddie - Diane's son. I Was invited but was afraid of the long 15-hour flight. Julia and Albert wanted to show the daughters their birthplaces. The first part of the 21 days was a tour, and they were on their own for the last 11 days. The Daughters saw the cities where they were born. One often-mentioned story was when Albert was a young boy; he had friends there; now, he is 72 years old. He walked up to men his age sitting on a park bench and told them he grew up there. They looked at him and listened to his recollection of the time there. One asked him if he had cut himself on his leg climbing a fence. Al said, "Yes." The guys recalled that they began to talk to him like long-lost buddies.

On tour, Julia and Al were sitting where she could see the speedometer of the bus. She sees 100 plus and begins to fear traveling 100 + miles per hour on the road. Julia tells Al and indicates she is scared of going this fast. Albert tells her that 100 means 100 meters per hour or 63 miles per hour; she relaxes.

Both parents had cousins who showed the visitors a great time. In addition, they had a video camera and took videos of many gatherings with music and drinking.

I followed their daily tour locations with a map. The day they returned on the long flight, a severe hurricane moved into the Atlantic. I see the plane's route, which seems to fly into the storm. The weatherman said we don't have to worry because the storm is over the Atlantic. I yelled, "NO SIR, MY WIFE IS FLYING INTO THAT STORM!" When I picked them up at the airport, I asked Ed, who had flown many times to France, how the flight was. He said he was afraid; he never saw the consoles above his head shake like those on that flight. His eyes told me it was a scary trip home.

Joanne's Second Trip To Italy

Joanne's second trip was with her granddaughter Julia's high school class in 2018. Jo, Julia, Carol, and Marge Bender (Carol's mother-in-law). It was during Kent Roosevelt's spring break. Joanne and Marge could not keep up with the young crowd and would sit and watch the group enjoy the sights. The grandmas said the boys and girls helped them a lot, which convinced the old folks to think twice about a trip with high school kids.

Joanne Working -Tallmadge Middle School

Joanne was a stay-at-home mother until Carol was in school. She obtained a job in 1974 as a lunchroom and study hall monitor in the Tallmadge School System. She had the "Hole" for detentions, where she met some of Christine's boyfriends. I talked to one of those guys, and he commented she knew him by heart. Jo only worked there a couple of years and was planning to work for a pension because she only had the basic amount for social security.

High School in Cuyahoga Falls

Joanne begins working as a study-hull monitor at the Cuyahoga Falls High School. Her days were the days a fireman worked as a fireman. They don't have a standard work schedule, so Joanne would work one day one week and three days another week. She also had the detention study hall after school, which was a bad assignment. I used to stand outside the room and keep kids from messing with the people in the room. The trick was for the monitor to move around the room and not sit at the desk. Kids sitting in the back would sneak out and sneak in at the end of the time for detention. I would catch a guy, and he would say he has to go to the restroom, and I would say, you need to be excused, "Get a pass!".

Her first full-time teacher aide job was in 1983 at Lincoln Elementary School. She loved the job, but her position was eliminated due to the reorganization of the elementary school. However, the teacher wrote a beautiful evaluation of Joanne's work with the young disabled students.

She was hired for the same position at Robert's because of her glowing evaluations by the teacher and Principal at Lincoln. She was glad to continue working toward the 20-year goal, even knowing this position would be for two teachers.

"Mrs. Sipka, can you help me?"

Joanne going to Roberts Middle School was a full-time assignment that was good for her and, more importantly, for Roberts. She was to help two teachers assigned to work with disabled children. Becky and Jeanann would tell everyone what a great job she did helping them. Joanne aimed to work in the Falls School system to achieve 20 years and retire. The two teachers would say how often they would hear, "Mrs. Sipka can you help me?"

She would come home and tell stories about how she helped someone with a difficult task for these special boys and girls. The kids would pick on each other, and she had to act as a counselor and referee to settle a dispute numerous times. She could have written a book on her experiences. Her facial expressions had to be controlled many times to help the kids through the issue. However, she relished these kids and helped them, and the kids loved her in return. At grocery stores, she would often be greeted by a student who was excited to see her.

There were several written comments about her when she retired in 2001. The first one is from Mrs. Jeananne Adkins. I can picture Joanne crying as she left the school that last day. Our family was there to help her celebrate the party after school that day. There were tears shed that day; I added a few. Our family was proud of Joanne.

My Experience With A Student Joanne Always Talked About

She talked a great deal about a young girl whose father I had in my machine shop class at the High School years before. I had to sit in an after-school detention hearing at the high school. This hearing determined whether a student who missed too many classes would be allowed to continue, with conditions, or fail the course. This young lady walks in, and I recognize her and know her problem. She keeps forgetting things like where her books are when they are under her desk. She has not participated in gym classes because she forgets her gym clothes. Before this gym class, she is in a study hall and places her gym clothes under her desk. When she goes to the gym, she forgets her clothes, can't take gym, and is credited with a missed class. The clothes are under her desk in the study hall.

She sits down, and teachers ask her questions. She mentions she doesn't have her clothes for the gym and thus is not given credit for that day. After the 13-day limit, she comes before this group. She leaves, and the talk is not to give her credit and give a grade of "F." I spoke up and told the story about her problem that my wife told me. A counselor mentioned this was her problem, and the verdict was she would be allowed to continue with help from the gym teacher. What Joanne told me helped her that day. The young lady's problem was presented to the staff, and provisions were made to help the girl.

First Wedding Anniversary

We could not celebrate our first wedding anniversary because of my military obligation. I had to serve two years in the Army Reserves, and the first two weeks included June 28. I asked for any reasons a guy could be excused; none fit my request. We had our celebration after I returned.

Second Wedding Anniversary

The second year in the Army Reserves was the same two weeks in June 1960, including June 28. We decided I should take summer school classes at KSU. I didn't have to go with my company, but I was assigned two weeks after the summer class ended. I had to drive myself to Fort Belvoir for those two weeks. That was better than being somewhere in Kentucky. I completed the two years of reserve duty and was now on two years of call.

Joanne celebrating her 50th birthday

We celebrate our 25th wedding anniversary at my Uncle Johnny and Aunt Helen's 50th Anniversary. They celebrated their 25th, the day of our wedding

A SPECIAL ANNIVERSARY DINNER AT A SPECIAL PLACE.

I don't remember the year, but I wanted to take her to this place as a surprise. I told her to dress casually and would leave at six o'clock. We drive to the "White Castle Restaurant" in Cuyahoga Falls. She told me she wanted a nice restaurant. I mentioned we ate there on the last day of our honeymoon because we watched our money, so why not relive that memory? Jo said any other day but June 28. I felt guilty doing this, but I planned to go to Red Lobster, because she could order the shrimp plater. There is never a doggie bag of shrimp when she has their shrimp.

50th WEDDING ANNIVERSARY

Picture of the two of us

Picture of the family

My wife and I approached our 50th wedding anniversary and wanted to celebrate the occasion differently. People usually go to dinner and then an open house gathering at their house.`I wanted something different, so I talked my wife into a hall reception with a meal, music, and an evening like our wedding reception 50 years ago in 1958, except now our daughters and grandkids would be there. At the Saturday mass at our church, the priest had us repeat our vows (I cried reciting the vows), and two grandchildren were our best man and maid of honor. We went to the hall and greeted the family and guests. We didn't have any liquor or beer because the priest said we would need a professional bartender and a police officer in the hall. A dish jockey provided the music, and he had access to all kinds of music with his computer instead of the 5- 6 piece band like we had at our wedding. I asked the DJ if he had any Spike Jones music. He had no idea who Spike Jones was but did locate some songs. We had the traditional dance where the bride and groom danced to a romantic song, and people watched. Spike Jones was a band that played a song as you would expect, but after a minute, the band would use bells, whistles, gongs, and strange noisemakers to accent the music. The band was part of the 1940s and 1950s periods. My wife and I are dancing close, looking at each other as a new bride and groom, when suddenly the music changes to "CRASH, BANG, WHISTLES, BELLS, AND LORD KNOWS WHAT ELSE!" for a good minute, then back to the slow, relaxing music. Very few people knew how Spike Jones played a song. When everyone heard the loud, unusual "MUSIC," they all stopped and looked at us. We now started to dance fast and move around like the typical movements of today's music. I noticed my grandkids and their faces as they listened to the music of "OUR" day. The whole crowd saw us and were surprised. The DJ loved the song and said he would use that if he had other jobs for older people for their parties.

> *NOTE: I would recommend using a computer to find a song by Spike Jones to hear how the music and the sound effects used. Our song was "Cocktails for Two."*

We gave away a miniature mantel clock with a decal on the back as a souvenir. We mentioned we didn't serve liquor and beer, and this is for that. Everyone commented the clock was much better than the drinks.

Life After Retirement

She had a list of things she wanted to do the first few weeks. One was to sleep in and turn off the alarm clock. Jo came up with a list of things she wanted us to do around the house. I didn't mind those jobs because we were together; just the two of us were both retired, and we were a couple again.

Enjoying time at the beach at Hilton Head Island – our unit is visible in the background. Each day ends when we walk to the water, step in a few inches, and kiss like the one on our first date. This time, the kiss is not a surprise to her.

Picture taken at Our Lady of Victory's pancake breakfasts

We started taking vacations at Hilton Head Island in 1991 and stayed at villas inland away from the Ocean. We decided to purchase two timeshare villas at Monarch at Sea Pines. Each year, the two weeks are around Father's Day; one unit is on a fourth floor with an ocean view. Joanne and I would sit there and talk about our family and life. The breeze and shade made it easy to take a nap. Before we obtained the ocean view, Joanne would spend time at a large outlet mall. When we had the ocean view unit, I asked her if she was going to the outlet mall. She replied, "I can go to the outlet mall in our area and now enjoy the view and sitting at the beach."

We did stay both weeks several times because they were back to back. The second week was in a different unit, not Ocean View. We both enjoyed sitting on the beach under the umbrella in our chairs, and as we returned to our villa, we would walk to the water, step in a few inches, look at each other, express our love for each other, and kiss. I would kid her; that was like the first kiss. She would look at me as she did on that first date.

We would eat out at least one time with the family. Food costs are expensive, and most of the time, those with us don't have much money. The place was the "Crazy Crab" at Harbor Town. Joanne never had to look at the menu; it was the shrimp plate.

I liked the "Crazy Crab's" hushpuppies. As we look at the menu, one or two baskets are placed on the table. I take a couple and wait for the drinks and main dish. I like to eat a couple after because they are so tasty. I look at the baskets, and they are empty; I ask the waitress for more, and she brings more. I look around and see the baskets empty again – NO HUSHPUPPIES. If my grandsons are there, they take care of the puppies. Next time, I asked the waitress to give the basket to me because we had people who liked it more than me. The lady presents me with the bill and a take-home container full of hushpuppies and tells me to hide them. At the villa, I hide them in the refrigerator behind items that are out of sight. The next day, I could taste a puppy, look and look, move things around, and not have a box of hushpuppies. I YELL, "What happen to the hushpuppies?" I hear, "Grandpa, they taste better the next day." The trick is for Joanne and me to go to the restaurant, bring some back, and hide the hushpuppies in our bedroom.

We all enjoyed the Monarch facilities and beach. There are 300 feet of beach at low tide, and at high tide, people can stay on the beach.

We were in our 60s when we started and did crazy things initially. Jo wanted to collect every shell and sand dollar in the ocean. She bought books about shells and ways to make all kinds of items for our house. The "Shell Shop" at Culignie Plaza was where we had to visit during a "Cloudy day" or after time at the beach. I would stay outside and wait because the shop was small and crowded.

SHE TRIED TO KILL ME (just kidding)

How did she try to kill me? We learned you wait for low tide and walk out to shoulder-deep water to get sand dollars and shells. Use your feet to find the surface of the dollar or shell. Dive down and get the item; it's as simple as that. We are walking, moving our feet around, and she feels one. Joanne can't dive down, and that's my job. I had trouble staying down and kept returning with no shell or dollar. Joanne has this idea. I will dive down, and she will hold my head and keep me down to get the shell. She finds one; down I go; she pushes me down; I grab the shell; she keeps her hand on my head; I want to return because I have the shell. I must force myself up and break the surface, gasping for air. Her first question was, "Did you get the shell?" I told her the next time; I would pinch her butt to let her know I got the shell or sand dollar

I TRIED TO KILL HER (just kidding)

She tells people I tried to kill her, too. We would rent two bikes for the week, and we could ride when we wanted. Joanne and I decided to go for our first ride. We took towels and water and set out. We would stop to look at the fabulous houses and wonder who could afford a home like that. It was an easy ride, just rolling along effortlessly. We went to the island's tip, about 4 miles from our villa. The return was difficult because we were heading into a strong wind. It was a struggle, and we had to stop several times to rest. Joanne yelled at me that I was trying to kill her going this far. I kept saying those high-rise buildings in the distance are where our place is. (I was not sure, but I had to say something). Finally, we returned, and she told everyone I tried to kill her by taking this long bike ride. We learned to check the wind direction first, head into the wind, and use the wind at our back for the return ride. We had that backward.

The staff at Monarch have daily activities for the families. One year, Joanne won a bottle of wine, which we consumed at a meal in our unit; the next day, she filled the bottle with sand, placed it in a closet at home, and was forgotten. I found it, spread half on her grave, and kept the other half for me.

The time at Monarch is perfect for us. We can be busy all day or sit under an umbrella at the beach. Our high-back chairs allow us to nap, which is so easy. There is a breeze and sun, and not crowded where we set up our chairs. We have met new friends and look forward to seeing them each year. My job is returning to the villa and bringing back snacks, drinks, and whatever we forgot. We spend time walking down the beach, holding hands, and mostly being quiet. Our comments are about the houses beyond the dunes. We don't ride the bikes like we used to, but we look for shells and sand dollars. Joanne will find two or three for souvenirs.

We have three weeks at Monarch, two in June, back to back, and near or around Father's Day. The third is the first week in September, near Labor Day. The bad part of this week is the hurricane season. We were there a couple of years ago and had to evacuate mid-week. I remember the signs telling us we were eight feet above sea level. When they mention ten-foot tides, I picture the car underwater. That week is the most relaxing for older folks because kids are in school.

The first week is the oceanfront on the fourth floor with a 120-degree ocean view. There is a roof, and we are out of the sun. I always thought we would see Africa looking straight ahead, but we are looking south because of the Island's location. We try to eat breakfast on the deck. One year at another villa, we had some food on the plate and went inside for something, and crows came and cleaned the plate. After several hours at the ocean, we nap on the deck. There are many pictures of us catching a few winks.

The second week in June is still on the property but back, and doesn't have the ocean view. The room arrangements are the same; the walk to the beach is through the nice landscaped pools and growth.

Another nice feature is taking a trolley to the famous Harbor Town with the lighthouse. You walk 200 feet to Sea Pines Beach Club and catch the open-sided trolley. It saves driving, and there is a nice ride past the many villas and houses. One year, when a couple of grandkids were four or five, I took them for a ride until they called me and said supper was ready. We rode 3 or 4 trips, and the kids liked it.

I mention Hilton Head, and people think – golf. Maybe so, but for us, it's sand and water. We did experience "Tubbing," and that was fun. There were five of us, and we positioned three on one tube and two on the other. I was in front, and Nicholas was behind me. It started to rain. The guy driving the jetski started slow and took off, crossing the wake, and Nickolas flew off. I was holding on and felt Nick fall. We turned around and picked up Nick. The driver gave us an extra long ride because no one was waiting for a ride. I told the driver, you have to pry my hands off the handle because I held on tight.

The drive to HHI takes eleven to twelve hours due to the 750 miles. Sometimes, we would leave on Friday after work, travel halfway there, and stay at a motel. I Remember we would pick up a daughter after work at five PM, start the drive, and stop somewhere in West Virginia. This stop would give us a few good hours on Saturday to enjoy the beach at Monarch. One bad thing about the drive was going through Charlotte, North Carolina. There can't be any other city with the worst traffic problem than Charlotte at five PM.

Eagles at Fort Myers

The eagles' nest is behind us.

Joanne began watching a program on the computer about the eagle nest in Fort Myers, Florida. An Insurance Company positioned several cameras on the nest 24 hours, 7 days a week. It showed a mother and father eagle hatched two or three eggs, and several cameras showed every minute. Joanne would sit and comment when some activity would happen. I would hear, "Come here, the father just brought back a fish." Another one was, "The eggs are beginning to crack!" then there was the exciting comment, "An owl is trying to take a baby, and the father eagle is protecting the baby." You could see the area and the owl waiting for a chance, but Daddy was right there. I would walk over and sit and watch it with her. I remember someone gave names to the birds, and later, they used numbers and letters; she liked names better.

We were in Fort Myers and drove the few miles to sit by the trees that housed the nest. That was exciting for Joanne and me. Next to this site is a church; benches are turned to face the trees that sheltered the nest. We were two of the many visitors from different states; total strangers would talk about how they watch at home, and many drove out of their way to see this site. I notice expensive cameras with lenses trained on the nest. I can imagine those individuals could take beautiful shots of the colorful eagles.

Field of Dreams

Sitting and watching the kids of all ages live a dream

Looking for "Shoeless Joe Jackson in the corn. I kidded Joanne. I was going
to take an ear of corn home for a sovereign. She didn't like that idea

This story involves me, but the six-day trip to the Field Of Dreams in Iowa was for Joanne, too. I saw an ad on Facebook from a man who wanted to play catch with a different person every day for one year. I contacted Bob Dyer from the Akron Beacon Journal and asked how to find this person. A few days later, Mr. Dyer called and said he found the guy in Missouri. Mr. Dyer liked the novel idea, and their conversation mentioned the ideal location would be on the Field of Dreams. When I heard "IOWA," I didn't think driving 600 miles, playing catch for one hour, and driving back was a good idea; I said "no" to the idea. Jo and I talked, and I mentioned Joanne has a cousin who lives in Mishawaka, Indiana, and I have an Army buddy who lives on a farm in the Quad City area we haven't seen in a long time. We could spend two days visiting Dolores, traveling to Dyersville, Iowa, playing catch one day, visiting Lloyd for two days, and returning home. We would have a six-day vacation. Telephone calls were made, and the crazy idea of me playing catch with a guy from Missouri on the Field of Dreams, just like Kevin Costner did in the movie, was set.

Our drive to Michawaka was quick and pleasant; finding Doloris's home was easy. Joanne enjoyed the time with Doloris, and it was non-stop talking with her cousin. I stayed out of the way and did a lot of listening and talking to Doloris's children and grandchildren.

Driving around Chicago is difficult because of all the highways and expressways. Joanne was the navigator, and we did get on the road we needed. We stopped at a toll booth, and we were on our way. We are driving 75 miles per hour on the third lane of a six-lane highway when we see a sign TOLL BOOTH one mile ahead. We had two choices: 1) drive past the toll booth or 2) cross three lanes of traffic, causing a hundred-plus car crash to pay the one-dollar toll. We decided to drive past the booth. We received a letter from the state of Illinois informing us we owed one dollar after we returned.

We stayed overnight in Dubuque, Iowa; the next morning, we drove the 30 miles to Dyersville and the Field of Dreams. Here is a national symbol that is in the middle of a cornfield. Bryant, Bob Dyer, Joanne, and I almost had the place to ourselves. The three of us took turns pitching and catching and spent time talking in the shade. Joanne took pictures and was part of the conversation.

The four hours went quickly, and we then drove to Quad City, Iowa, and visited Lloyd Whitsell, a retired farmer. Lloyd's three children are the same age as our three daughters, and our families exchanged visits during the earlier years. This time, we met Lloyd's new wife, Margaret. Lloyd's first wife, Wanda, died 15 years ago. Jo had long talks with Marge, and Lloyd and I talked farm.

Our six-day vacation ended, and that crazy idea worked out nicely. We thought about stopping at Dolores's house on our way home, but Joanne said Dolores told her she was sick and didn't have much time. Dolores died two months after our visit, and Joanne was happy she talked with her for those few days.

Class of 1954

Joanne graduated from Cuyahoga Falls High School in 1954. She had a list of 20 girls from that class who formed a club after the ladies' families grew up. They would meet once a month at noon for lunch or a picnic when the weather was nice. Jo would attend and enjoy seeing her old girlfriends. That day is marked on the calendar because the get-together was important. She would spend time telling me what was said and the latest news when she returned.

Joanne enjoyed her class reunions, and we didn't miss too many. It was nice because the city had just one high school, and all attended. I would usually find another husband, sit, and watch the girls move around and enjoy themselves.

One reunion was worth mentioning. The event was to be held at the Holiday Inn hotel in Akron. At the same time, a "swinger's party" was also scheduled on a different floor. The City of Akron wanted to stop that event but couldn't. So, both activities took place. The class president made some comical comments about both events at the opening of the reunion. I remember one like, "Well, class, we made everyone think this was a class reunion; we fooled them! Didn't we?" Many knew what the class president was talking about, but soon, those from out of town found out, and there were many comments.

The 50th reunion was a big event in 2004 at the hotel in Cuyahoga Falls. One reunion was scheduled on a cruise ship; we didn't make that one because it was during the time we were staying with Joanne's mom.

Slot Machines (computers)

She could use a computer for her emails, paying bills, and entertainment (slot machines). She would play the slot machines, yell when she hit the jackpot, and tell how many coins she won. I asked her to convert the winnings to real money. One day, something happened, and she lost all her coins. You would think it was real money. She would yell when she hit a big pot and tell me the amount. I would yell, "Cash it in for real money!

Real Slot Machines

Joanne was a cool, calm person, except near a real slot machine. We visited a couple of gambling places and played the slots. At first, we would play side-by-side, but after, we would separate because I would win a few coins, and she would reach in and take my winnings. We would be in different aisles so I could keep my coins. *NOTE: these experiences were with the old fashion coin machines.*

Once, We were on a ferry gambling ship in Quad City, Illinois, visiting Lloyd and Wanda. I walked away and saw a $5 machine. I looked around for Jo; I didn't see her and purchased 3 $5 coins. The coins went in, and I walked away with nine coins. Joanne was sitting at the rear of the paddlewheel ship with our friends, and I placed the nine heavy coins in her lap. Our lady friend yelled, "Those are $5 coins!" Jo chewed me out for playing such an expensive machine. I replied that I started with three and now have nine, each worth $5. Joanne grabbed them, and we cashed them in for $45. I told her I made sure she wasn't around to steal and play the slugs.

The IPAD for CHRISTMAS

"The iPad was one gift she enjoyed too much. This gift did cause arguments because she would forget the time of day. Jo was so engrossed in the games that I had to remind her that it was 11:00 or later. When there was a problem, she quickly called a grandchild to help fix the problem. I would tell people the one finger on her right is very strong and don't "Finger" wrestle her with that finger. Once, the connector plugged into the unit broke; she insisted I get another one.

Christmas and Other Holidays

The girls dressed up for Christmas

Pictures of girls by the fireplace

Both of our families always celebrated the holidays big time. Joanne's family was the main source of holiday activity because my mom lived with my sister Helene in Florida. My family would have a large party at a restaurant where we would have games and share gifts. It was a lot of fun. Christmas was the busiest for all the family as food and cookies were baked for Christmas. That continued in our family. I remember Joanne and me making several kinds of cookies and nut rolls. We had a special wooden board that her mother had used for years. One of my jobs was to grind the walnuts for the nut roll and chop the nuts for other cookies. I loved these jobs because I was the "Official" tester of the cookies and rolls. I always said I had to taste another one to determine if that item was okay. It took us three or four days to complete the cookies and rolls. We both felt good doing this for our family and hoped this tradition would continue. No one is married, so maybe the practice may stop.

Caplets for Christmas

Making Caplets was a family event. Jo and I prepared the meat and chicken and usually scheduled a Sunday to make these special noodles. Our dining table would have five or six chairs where an individual would have a plate, take the round piece of thin dough, place a small portion of meat on the dough, and fold it a certain way. Another person would bag 50 of these in a freezer bag. Two or three others would handle the large piece of dough, cut it into smaller pieces, and run it through a device that would squeeze it into a thin piece of dough. A special tool would be rolled over the dough, cutting out the small round pieces. Joanne was the one who would add the ingredients to the bread maker. Julia (our granddaughter) began to want this job. She wrote down the items needed and was the one who took this job for the last two years.

The group sitting there would enjoy socializing about this and that. Diane, Ed, and their son Eddie would come and spend time doing different jobs. We would order pizza and drinks and spend six to seven hours making around 800 caplets. When Joanne was here, she would start, sit in the kitchen, listen, and enjoy the activity. We could have watched a Cleveland Browns football game if it was a Sunday.

We would make 800 to 850 and place them in the freezer for Christmas dinner. We would hide two or three bags under other items to have caplets after the holidays. I hope the family isn't too upset finding this out.

A couple of days ago, Carol brought a soup container with caplets. I guess someone else also took a bag or two. It tasted good, and I wished there was more, but enough to think of Christmas. (*can you keep a secret? There is one more package left in our freezer*)

Mother's Day 2019

Becoming Grandparents

Our family consisted of three girls, Jo and me, but the girls married and had children, which provided a new title: GRANDPARENTS or GRANDMA and GRANDPA. The added title affected Jo more than me. Her involvement with the girls when they were pregnant was outstanding; it was a dream come true. Each grandchild was told they were grandma's favorite, and they never argued between themselves.

Angela, Our Angel in Heaven

Our Angel in heaven

Christine was pregnant and in the hospital, trying to keep the baby from an early delivery. The projected birth date was after the first of January 1988. Joanne and Dave (Chris's husband) would take turns staying with Chris. Sunday, September 27, 1987, we get a call that Chris gave birth. We rushed to the hospital and saw a beautiful baby girl who weighed three pounds and a few ounces and was in an isolette. The baby would be transported to Akron Children's Hospital. Christine looked like that when she was born, and Jo and I mentioned this feature. We left after a few hours and said we would return in the evening. We were happy but concerned about the baby's weight, so we returned. Family members were told the good news, and Jo and I prepared to return early evening to enjoy looking at our tiny baby girl.

No one can imagine the change in a person's feelings that we experienced when we saw our baby girl in the isolette with tubes everywhere attached to tanks and gages. Dave, Joanne, and I were told the baby took a turn for the worse and was near death. Pure happiness and, in one second, total deep sorrow. I stood there stunned, thinking there must be something to do to counter the wrong. Why aren't the staff doing these things? I turned away and cried as I had never done before. Would you please do something? I wanted to yell but could see the doctors telling us why this happened and what they tried. I could not hear anything they said. I walked away and slowly walked past many little baskets with babies inside. I noticed them and wondered why our baby was. Joanne stayed and was able to hold our grandchild for a while. She said that was the worst moment of her life and blamed herself for that tragedy. Jo would recall those memories many times when she was down and upset. We said we must get to heaven because we will be with our angel forever. I believe Angela was the first person Joanne saw when she passed into heaven.

Julia also talked to Joanne and mentioned that she had problems, too, and didn't take any drugs. Her comment was, "That is how we are made!"

Christine and Dave divorced soon after. Chris then adopted Katie in 2002.

Grandma Jo's Best Work Was For and With The 8 Grandkids

We became grandparents with the birth of Angela on Sept 27, 1987. but began to experience being a grandparent again with the birth of Justin in 1990. I appreciate my grandkids, but Joanne's love exceeds my feelings. I was concerned about world problems, while Joanne was concerned about particular issues about every daughter and grandchild. I was planning to write several paragraphs about her being a grandma but decided to include the stories from the family and friends.

Each family member wrote something about Grandma Joanne. I didn't know most of the stories, but I understood how they occurred. I can say there was a special look on Jo's face when she was with a grandchild. They would always give her a kiss when they would leave. Me? Maybe say, "Goodnight, Grandpa!" I would hear her say time and time again, "I could just squeeze them to death!" At times, I would say, "What about me?" She would say, "You already had your kiss!"

We wanted to include family in our trips to Hilton Head Island and be with them for that week. I loved the way she loved our family. Her look was priceless!

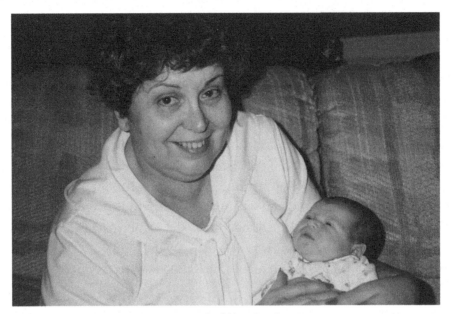

Joanne holding Justin

Joanne holding Corey

All the grandkids taking a nice picture

One of Grandma's birthdays. She said the birthday is better with the grandkids

From left to right, Grandma, Mackenzie (Monica's friend), Monica, Joey, Corey, Nicholas, and Grandpa at Hilton Head Island, ready to go to the Crazy Crab to eat.

I tried to help in the "grandpa way," but it did not compare to Joanne's. I remember driving Jo to many homes, watching her involve herself, and enjoying every minute. When she returned home, Grandma would sleep well that night or stay up worrying about some issues.

The following are stories from the family and friends about Joanne.

Diane (Braghieri) Kempton – Joanne's Sister

Joanne was my sister for 77 years, and I dearly loved her. Joanne was a good daughter to our parents. She was a caring sister to me and a protected and loving mother to her daughters.

Joanne was a good student in school and had many friends. We loved spending all holidays together.

Christine - Daughter Number One

Here's one example of the love my Mom and Dad had. We eat dinner at the dinner table together every night. There was always a home-cooked meal every night for us. I remember Thursday was spaghetti, Friday was fish. After we ate, it was time that my Mom and Dad had together to watch TV. My Mom would sit on the couch, and my Dad would sit on the floor in front of her so she could scratch his back. We girls had jobs, wash the dishes, and feed the dog. Carol usually dried the dishes, or she would say "I'm" tired.

I would always tell my Mom she was lucky to have Dad because there is no one like him. She would smile and say, and I'm very loved.

Cathy - Daughter Number Two

Mom had a secret addiction, and to this day, I was sworn to keep her secret. I know she understands why I can now break my vow of silence and share this memory with everyone. I am sure Mom is laughing and smiling in heaven as I share this special memory of her.

Her secret was ………

Mom was a self-proclaimed <u>chocoholic.</u> She craved chocolate and would do anything to find it and eat it throughout the day.

One day while Mom was staying with me and caring for me during my second pregnancy, I told her how thirsty and hungry I was and that I craved water and chocolate. She nodded her head and then looked surprised upon hearing my requests. My water craving was understandable to Mom due to experiencing dehydration and having pregnancy complications called hyperemesis gravdarum, where I had severe nausea, vomiting, and weight loss. She experienced the same complications with her pregnancies and knew that I couldn't keep liquids and solids down so I had to be thirsty. However, she seemed surprised with the thought of my chocolate craving since I was so physically weak and sick. Mom heard my request but quickly tried to distract me from my wishes by changing the subject. She said, "Cathy, you know you can only have small amounts of a bland carbohydrate or protein food, and unfortunately, chocolate isn't one of those Miss Cathy, the Dietitian!" We both laughed even though I wanted to cry. I knew I couldn't tolerate chocolate in my stomach at this point in the pregnancy, but I was craving it. I pleaded with her and explained that I was having dreams about my pre-pregnancy days where I would buy M&M's or any piece of chocolate to help and eat them(or ration them out) while studying. One M&M reward per page of homework when reading or memorizing a flashcard. There was nothing like a piece of chocolate to help me relax and feel great. It sure sounded good that day. After I told her about my chocolate craving and adventures, she laughed and said,

"Oh Thank You, God! I feel better now that I can get this off my chest. I can finally share my secret addiction with someone. What a relief…. Especially since you have the same addiction, Cathy!"

She said she once climbed up on the kitchen counter and searched the top cabinet shelf of several baking items until she found a half bag of semi-sweet Nestle chocolate morsels to eat to get her through her chocolate craving that day. She laughed and said that she obviously needed to keep more chocolate in the house as she had to ravage the house looking for chocolate chips that were supposed to be in cookies. Usually, she said she always had some chocolate stashed away just in case she needed it, and she made sure Dad had no idea where her secret stash was in the house. I laughed and said, "No way, Mom! I do the same thing!" Then we both laughed and said at the same time, "I guess, We're just Crazy Chocoholics! Don't mess with our Chocolate Stash!:

She said It's OUR SECRET. Don't tell a soul! I promised her that day that our secret was safe with me. Yes, safe until today.

CATHY'S SECOND STORY

Some of my most cherished moments and memories of Mom were from when she helped me and my family during my pregnancies. She spent hours, days, and weeks by my bedside, being my own private nurse, and then also prepared my foods along with household chores and "Grandmaing" my boys while I lay in bed getting through some of the most painful, miserable, exhausting and weak moments of my life. From the moment I found out I was pregnant, she started planning how she could rearrange her life to help me because she truly knew I needed her and her help to get through each *day during the first several months of each pregnancy. She even moved to my home in Tennessee to help me through my second pregnancy.*

She had the same experience with difficult pregnancies, and so did her Mom. We both believed that our Mom's were so important in helping us through this time in our lives. She would say," all this suffering and Pain will be forgotten the moment you hold this Little Sweetheart Baby Cathy, Love You" Mom had the patience of a saint while comforting me as a woman who experienced the same difficult pregnancies. She knew the pregnancy condition was real and kept me focused on getting past the endless vomiting and dehydration of each pregnancy (frequent admission to the hospital for IV nourishment).

She prepared countless foods just for me to try. Mom had this gentle, caring motivation way of encouraging me to try little bits of food just to provide nourishment to me and the baby or, according to her, "Our Little Sweetheart." She was dedicated to being the Best Nurse to me; I am forever indebted to her

Mom would describe her nursing duties and then tell me that my job was to focus on resting and laying still to keep nutrients (food) down instead of stressing about who could care for my boys when my husband wasn't home. I could count on her to be the best Grandma-Substitute Mom to my boys when I couldn't lift my head off the pillow from sickness.

Without her help, I wondered if I could make it through the day. She was my rock. My strength and courage while I lay in bed. The rock that I hope to be for my boys and family every day. There were so many moments that she sat by my side to pray, cry, talk, and laugh while holding my hand to ease my pain, then would say "Love You" before she left the room to help around the house with the boys. Knowing she was doing my job with the boys was the most reassuring and motivating feeling that I could have had during those difficult times. I know her actions exemplified the best qualities of an excellent nurse. She didn't need a diploma or a college degree to prove she was a nurse because her life and her help with me showed us all what a Great Nurse truly is. Mom was the Best Nurse a daughter could ask for.

She was there for so many happy moments and helped me get through fighting, determined, desperate attempts to carry a baby into this world. She would encourage me by reminding me that each day was another day to normalcy or being a normal pregnant Mom. This is where I could do the normal things pregnant Moms do again with my boys. I believed in her. I knew she made it through her pregnancies with healthy babies, and I could make it too!

<u>"I have been the Nurse I always wanted to be, after all."</u>

Mom always wanted to be a nurse, and I know she felt bad that she wasn't able to finish Nursing school. She did make comments at times about how her life might have been different if she was a Registered Nurse.

I believe she was that Nurse to me and so many others during her life. She went from helping one family member to another. She had all the nursing attributes of caring, giving, nurturing, and helping others her entire life. The day after her hip surgery, we were talking about how great she felt and that she was going to get better soon, so I could have my hip surgery also, and she could help me. She was already planning to take care of me (someone else) before she even recovered from her own surgery. She had that selfless concern about the needs of others over her own,

I know Mom and I talked after everyone left her room that day about how she finally felt she was the Nurse she always wanted to be. She even admitted to being a good one because of the years of experience with the doctors and care she provided to her Mom. She said

> *"Cathy, I helped so many people when I worked at the Pediatrician's office, and my nursing care was respected by all the doctors there. I was Grandma's nurse for thirteen years and would do anything to help you girls."*

I commented to her that she took immaculate care of Nonnie and me and treated us like queens. She smiled and said

> *"Yes, I guess I did do this nursing thing right after all. I don't need a diploma on the wall to prove this."*

I remember after she made that comment, I felt she finally agreed and was reassured that she made the right life career choice. Maybe she wasn't an official nurse by degree but worked as a nurse in her daily life for so many years. After she made that comment, it seemed like what I call "Quiet Peace" in the room to me as we talked about her actual career choices (Teachers' Aide and Study hall monitor). The room seemed so surreal. Mom seemed content and proud. I was proud of her and that our whole family was proud of her too! She was the most caring woman I have ever known, The conversation and realization wasn't meant to be a lifetime mom/daughter talk, but it ended up being out last real mom/daughter talk. See, Mom was admitted to the hospital later that evening and remained there until she took her last breath months later.

She would thank Dad, Chris, Carol, and I for staying with her in the hospital all those hours, days, and months. We all three girls vowed to make sure we were with her at all times and that she wasn't alone in the hospital. We tried to be the Nurse to her that she was to us during our lifetime... We just need more time... We ran out of time to help her...

She continued to be selfless and grateful through to the very end and would thank me for staying through the night with her at the hospital. I would respond with tears and say, Mon, this is nothing compared to all you did for me in my lifetime, Love you".

Today, I miss her so much and pray to her every day. I tell her that I wish I could have been the nurse to her that she was to me and our family in my prayers.

I will always remember the beautiful moments of our life, Mom "All the times you were by my side, whether it be...by my bed, or in the stands, holding my hand or holding my babies, laughing with joy or crying in pain and heartache, or watching my boys" "Love You!"

I know you are still watching over us now from Heaven above. Thank You for your Nurturing Love and Care. You helped us all with Enduring Selfless Love, Care, and Tenderness.

You were truly the Best Nurse!

Love you so much, Mom
Cathy

Carol – Daughter Number Three

When I think about the best memories of my mom, it will not be what everyone would think. You see, when my mom was in the hospital before she went to heaven, we had some of the best talks about our lives as mother and daughter. We talked about all the funny things that happened to us. We decided that I should have never dressed myself that one Sunday morning before church. How I missed my first day of kindergarten and first day of college (not due to the same reason). Being roommates on our trip to Italy and seeing all the beautiful churches.

She also was my biggest supporter when I was unsure of the outcome. Wanting to be with me for all my babies being born and giving me a shoulder and hugs for the ones I will meet when I go to heaven. Going with me on December 23rd, 1992, and holding my hand so I could have Monica. Driving an hour in the blizzard 1995 to watch Monica so I could take Joey to the hospital for jaundice treatments. Reassuring me that Julia would be OK after some serious test that were not expected. And when we almost lost Melissa, she let me use her shoulder, and I knew she would make sure I could be with her and others, and the others would be safe and taken care of.

The hardest part of our talks in the hospital were that these might be our last talks we might have, so my sisters and I decided to make sure she would never be alone during these times. Our night talks, because I would stay the nights, were full of smiles, tears and lots of hand squeezes knowing we will always stay together no matter where we go. I will always be her baby and loved it when she would say, "This is my baby."

Justin Spicer (30) – Grandkid #1

Justin was our second grandchild, and Joanne was a happy grandmother helping Cathy. She found a new life, and her happiness was obvious. We have recordings of Jo and Justin, age 2, talking at our dining table. She would comment to me how she could just squeeze those kids.

I remember being woken up early to go to swim practice even though I didn't want to go. I would pretend to be sleeping in the car and not have to practice, and then after practice, me and Corey would walk from Water Works through the park across the street over to your house. Grandma would always cook us breakfast (eggs, cheese, and sausage).

I also remember when I would come and cut the grass, Grandma would always have a cold $1 Arizona Ice Tea waiting for me when I would take a break.

I remember always finding her in the stands at different sporting events and loved that she would always come out and support all of the Grandchildren. Sometimes, she would give me advice, and I was like, "Grandma, where did you hear/learn that."

I remember how she would always laugh when me and Monica would fake like we were drinking wine at Thanksgiving or Christmas dinners.

I loved that she kept up with watching the live stream of the Bald Eagles hatching and loved to play her Facebook Candy Crush games (she even beat me a few times)

She was such a big part of our family and is deeply missed, but I know she is still watching over all of us and cheering for us from the sky!

Monica Sincel, (28) – Granddaughter #2

The 40 miles drive to Carol's house was not a problem. Monica was the first girl grandchild and was born in the Youngstown, Ohio area.

There are still days that go by where I forget that she's passed. I have to remind myself all over again of everything that happened. There are five stages of grief, the first one being "denial and isolation." I often find myself wondering if I am still stuck in that stage. I have little glimpses of those final months; everything that was said, facial gestures, hand holding, tears, hugs, every hospital room, music and sounds, all of which will never be forgotten. All of my senses were dialed up to a 10, and I remember all of it. I still have the playlist that I made for her when she was in the hospital, and I still listen to it from time to time. I think I'm still in disbelief, and I'm not sure I'll ever get out of this place. And I think that's why It's taking me so long to finally write something. I literally don't know where to begin.

A large chapter of my childhood was pretty difficult. I saw a lot of people I love hurt each other, make each other cry, say things they didn't mean, and even worse, say things they did mean. Everyone around me was changing because of all these terrible circumstances, everybody but my grandma. At the time, I only knew a couple phone numbers by heart, and those were for my grandma's house. Anytime I would witness something, find something, hear anything, I would call her. She was always the voice of reason during that time when I simply couldn't understand what was going on. She was always a constant calm presence during this time that was absolute chaos. She always knew exactly what to say to help me.

Flash forward to college; I personally was going through a lot of changes in my life. My health, new relationships, friendships, college swimming, and academics. I was in a situation where there was a lot of change in my life, but good change. Once a week or once every two weeks, I will call my grandma and talk to her about everything. It's amazing how fast 30 minutes on the phone can go, then you blink, and it's been an hour. She was always so wise and calm about everything. I really admired that about her. I really admire that in any Italian woman, really. There were moments during this time where I realized that nobody understands me like my grandmother does, not even my parents.

I remember when she passed away. I was going through a really terrible break up one that left me crying day in and day out. I was a mess. I couldn't hold it together and I felt very alone during that time. One day I was having a moment in my bedroom crying in my bed. Suddenly, I had this sudden urge to look through all of my old birthday cards. I think I wanted to find her signature. As I was looking through all of the cards, I found an envelope with my name and address to the college house I was living in. It was a three-page letter from my grandma. One that she wrote me when I was going through a break six years ago. How is it that in that moment I was led to find that letter? Is it possible my grandma led me to that letter? I like to think yes, it was little moments like that after she passed that started to open my eyes to everything around me. It's little moments like that, ones I still get today, that I know she is still involved in my life. Little winks from heaven. These little winks from heaven have helped my grief and helped open up a new chapter of my relationship with my grandmother. One that I know is still present and in my life every day.

Corey Spicer, (26) – Grandkid #3

Cathy's Corey was next, and he was born in Nashville, Tennessee. We drove there, and Joanne stayed there for five weeks and loved every minute. NOTE Cathy included a story about mom and the surprising acknowledgment from Joanne.

Nothing like being able to give your grandma a touchdown for her birthday in one of the biggest games Kent Roosevelt high school has played. It wasn't something I could have ever dreamed of, seeing I played mainly defensive end my junior year. But something about the game felt different going into the Kent State Stadium on a brisk fall night. I couldn't put my finger on it at the time. Just figured it was the nerves building up for the big game. This was going to be the first time in a long time Kent Roosevelt would host a "Home" playoff game. Seeing the high school field wasn't in playing condition after a full season and a lot of rain, the game was moved a couple of miles down the road to Kent State. This amplified the nerves a bit getting to play in a college football stadium in your hometown. Luckily it would still be in front of our home crowd and families. Going through the pregame warm-ups, I could feel something different than all the previous games. They say things happen for a reason, so I guess this was just my warning of something big to come. The game started, and we got smacked in the mouth on their first drive of the game; Ellet scored. The quick TD was something no one really expected to happen since our defense had been strong all year long. Following that drive, on our first pass of the game, our All-State Quarterback was intercepted. I remember thinking, "oh boy, this is not good." The defense would hold for the next couple of plays. Then I would understand why I had this strange feeling all day long. Ellet's quarterback would scramble to his right due to pressure up the middle and deliver the perfect pass right into my hands across the middle of the field. With a couple of blockers in front of me and some open field, it was off to the races for a 90-yard touchdown. The Kent stands were the loudest I've ever heard them as I made my way to the sidelines. After some congratulations from my teammates and some water, I looked up to find my family in the crowd of people. It wasn't too hard to find them, seeing they were acting the craziest out of everyone. We ended up going on to win 24-7. I was pretty relieved when it was over, and I got to see my family after the game. <u>"Thank you for the Birthday Touchdown"</u> was the first thing I heard after my grandma gave me a big hug. Safe to say she liked her present

I have to add a story about this big day for Corey and Joanne. In the stands, a lady offered me a chance to buy six tickets for the 50-50 raffle; I said "no." The lady behind me bought <u>that</u> strip of tickets. Yes! She won the 50-50 and over $300. Grandma was happy, and I was <u>sad</u>.

Joe Sincel, (26) – Grandson #4

Carol had Joey, and there were problems at birth. Again Joanne was there to help and never complained about what she had to do. Joe was born in December, and the weather did cause problems; one was she had to drive in a snowstorm, which worried her.

One of my fondest memories of my Grandma was when we went to Hilton Head Island. We would watch a movie after a day of playing in the sun to relax. We watched "Dinner for the Smuckers." She was not familiar with the movie, and the way she laughed will always be something. I remember she giggled, and we all loved to see her happy that way.

Another memory of grandma was her always making sure we had something to eat whenever we came over.

When we were all little, the hugs and her kisses were all we needed until we saw her again.

Julia Sincel, (24) – granddaughter #5

Carol gave birth to Julia in May, and again Joanne was there to help.

The Pink Ladies

In March of 2015, I got the privilege of going to Italy with my Mom, my Grandma Bender (Granny), and My Grandma Sipka (Grandma). I had other classmates and teachers on this trip as well, as it was technically a school excursion that family was allowed to join. It was quite a successful expedition, and everyone had an amazing time, but it was especially memorable for me with all of my classmates helping out the "pink ladies." Both Grandma and Grammy had lovely pink jackets on, and everyone could point them out from a mile away! Although they couldn't always come along on the more physically demanding excursions, they always found someplace to look around, and by that, I mean a church to light a candle in. If we couldn't find them, we knew just by looking up the nearest church, and we were one step closer. On the first day that we visited the Vatican, I remember everyone was so excited for the "Pink Ladies" to get to see St. Peters basilica. The whole trip they had been in of these small, local churches, and now they were going to get to see the largest catholic church in the world. Remember walking in with my Grandma, Grammy, and my mom and seeing The Pieta at the same time. We were struck by its beauty and stood there and talked about how shocking it was to see in person. For those who don't know, The Pieta is a Renaissance sculpture by Michelangelo Buonarroti. It depicted the Virgin Mary holding Christ in her arms after he was crucified. Mary is known for being strong-minded and courageous, so it came by no surprise that all of us women were in awe of this piece and her beauty. It was something I have seen pictures of many times, but they truly do it no justice. The next day my family and I were lucky enough to return to the Vatican again to get a "behind the scenes" tour. We saw the Sistine Chapel, where the pope stays, and even talked to someone in the Swiss Guard. But I remember eating lunch that day and telling my grandma The Pieta was still my favorite part of not only the Vatican but of all of Italy. It was one of the most beautiful things I had ever seen, and I got to share that moment with three amazing women in my family.

Katie Simmons, (22) – Granddaughter #6

Chris adopted Katie at the age of three, and Chris being a single mom, required Joanne's help

Joanne, my Grandma, was a wonderful person. I am so glad I got to be in her life. I will always remember all the times we went to Hilton Head Island and Christmas times, laughs, smiles, and hugs.

I will always cherish the days I would come over, and there would be either a ton of zucchini loaves in bags or a ton of cookies. Those were the good memories of her I will forever keep in my heart.

My Grandma was one of my biggest supporters. She will always hold a special place in my heart. LLG

One of the things I vividly remember about my grandma and stuff us doing was going to our local Kmart, whether for school items or outfits for school or getting a baby shower gift. We walked around the store trying on shoes or buying certain pairs of shorts. I miss my grandma and Kmart and hope there is a Kmart in heaven for my Grandma.

One of the ways my grandma was able to relax her mind was by playing on her iPad. I could relate, so I always encouraged her to use it whenever she needed more coins for bingo or needed an extra life. I would send it to her on facebook because I knew how important it was to her so I always made sure to help her if and when I could. I remember when the iPad wasn't working (ex. Screen not turning on), she would call me Saying," Katie, my computer isn't working!" I would rush over there and hold down the power, home, and low volume buttons to restart it, and she would be so happy when it would come back on. She would thank me and continue to say, "I thought I broke the computer." I would always reassure her that I would always be able to help with her iPad problems. I miss going over to help with those problems.

NOTE – Joanne and her sister Diane met in 2017 and worked out their difference when they met at a restaurant. Katie talked to Jo and Diana several times and became sisters again instead of being estranged.

Nicholas Spicer, (22) – Grandson #7

Nicholas (Cathy's son) is the last boy and was born in Akron, Ohio.

There are a bunch of memories I have with her. One that sticks out the most would have to be my senior year of high school, and our last swim meet at home. We did the senior walk and then took pictures with our families. I remember her shedding a tear or two and giving me a big hug with her beautiful smile she always had. I told her not to shed a tear; it's a celebration even though I know it was a big deal to our family. She took the picture right next to me and didn't let go of the hug. It was a celebration that all the Spicer boys finished their sporting careers at Theodore Roosevelt High School. Every sporting event my Grandpa and Grandma attended, even if they had things to do. They were there for us boys. That memory will stick with me forever. On the sidelines, while I'm coaching sports, teaching in the classroom, or just at home with my family. The loving spirit of her lives in me and will forever be a part of my life.

Melissa Sincel (21) – Granddaughter #8

Carol gave birth to Melissa in September, and Joanne was helping and enjoying every minute.

One of my earliest memories with Grandma Joanne is when she would watch me after school and we would sit and watch the jewelry channel. I remember we would watch the women present the different jewelry pieces and talk about what we liked and which we wanted. I haven't been able to understand why that memory is one of the only memories I have around that age, but I think it was the feeling of closeness being snuggled up next to her and the bonding in spending that special time with her.

The next thing I remember with grandma that I loved so much was that grandma was the person that you could go talk to all the time. She loved to listen to stories about our day, and she had the best reactions about the smallest things. The jokes were hilarious, and the crazy moments were insane. She listened so well that talking to her about stuff was almost like therapy.

Another memory I have of grandma is the small gifts I would get from her. She's given me some of the dolls she had and collected, and another time she gave me a necklace she loved. She loved to give things that meant so much to her because I meant so much to her, and looking at those things every day just reminds me of that. I definitely wish grandma had been able to make it through her procedure and that she would still be here today, but I have to have faith that things happen for a reason and maybe going when she did spare her from a lot more pain later. I choose to believe that grandma is happy spending time with her mom and dad and all the lost babies in our family. I know she's missing grandpa Stan and her daughters and grandchildren, but I know she's with all of us as our guardian angel, and she sees us every day. When I'm sad, I picture her in the passenger seat of my car, or sitting on the couch in my living room, or standing behind me with her hands on my shoulders. I know she's with me everyday, and she will be for the rest of my life, which is why I work hard everyday to become a woman who will make her proud.

Marilyn Barber – a close friend of Joanne

The following is a letter from Marilyn Hagerman, Barber, a close friend of Joanne. Their friendship extends into grade school. (Marilyn's comment 04/13/21)

Joanne always had such a good heart. When she was first married and working for Dr. Rogers, she volunteered to give my mom a vitamin shot in her hip. Jo would come weekly after work for almost a year. She always had a smile and a happy attitude even after a long and many times frustrating day. How lucky we were to have her.

Joanne had a surprise baby shower for our first child in 1971. It was appreciated.

Mrs. Sue Wells Next-Door Neighbor

Joanne and I became friends after she moved into the house next door to help care for her mother, Julia (of course, she brought Stan along with her). Julia was a spunky Italian woman. We became buddies and even went through cancer together. As a woman in her 80's, twice my age, she inspired me.

I thought if she can endure cancer and treatment, I can too. When Julia and I visited, Joanne would join in our conversation and enjoyed our time together.

Through, the years Julia became less talkative, but Joanne and I did not. We developed a special friendship. And when Julia passed Joanne and I became even closer friends.

Whenever Joanne answered the door, she always had a smile on her face and made me feel welcomed. Never did she make me feel like I was intruding. Also, she took time for me and wasn't too busy to have a girlie chat. Her kindness made me feel at ease and we could comfortably discuss any topic. However, as a devoted wife, mother, and grandmother, her favorite topic was her family.

I often think about one-on-one intimate conversations are all that is needed for a meaningful friendship. Joanne and I never went to lunch together, a movie, or shopping. Our relationship revolved around two comfortable pieces of furniture and two people who loved and cared about each other.

Our relationship began in a living room, and we spent our last moments together in a hospital room. Joanne was unconscious, and her family took shifts to be at her bedside, so she was not alone. I was asked to cover a shift, and I was honored. I didn't hesitate to say "yes" so I could spend some time with a dear friend.

I took a CD player and found some songs that I thought might be uplifting for Joanne, such as Amazing Grace. I held her hand and talked to her just like I always did about what was going on in my life and included that Stan was trying to behave himself. I know Joanne could hear me, and I hope my visit helped provide a peaceful atmosphere and maybe a few chuckles.

I'm thankful for my friendship with Joanne. She set a wonderful example of the meaning of hospitality. I miss her, but I know that she is no longer suffering, and I will see her again.

Comments From the Staff of Roberts at Joanne's Retirement Party

Letter from Jeanne Aikens

Joanne Sipka was my friend, my "big sister" and my teacher's aide. I met Joanne on my first day at Robert's Middle School. I was hired as an LD Tutor. Our secretary introduced Joanne to me after which Joanne very graciously helped me overcome my first hurdle with returning to the classroom. She showed me how to use the photocopier after having been away from teaching since the days of the mimeograph or "ditto" machine. This was the first day of always gracious and willing, never complaining, help that I received from Joanne for the next sixteen years. She was an aide in the Learning Disabilities class at the time.

It was another two years until I became a fulltime classroom teacher in one of the two Developmentally Handicapped units that now shared Joanne as an aide. She had double duty, so to speak. She spent her days assisting with instruction, as directed, in both classrooms. Joanne assisted teaching all the subjects, usually in a small group setting. She instructed the whole class if needed on occasion. She prepared students for tests, helped with assignments from other teachers, accompanied students to Art, Music, Home Economic and Industrial Arts, escorted students in the hallway to class, assisted physically impaired students and passed medications. Of course a great deal of her time was spent on special projects and preparation of materials. The most time consuming for Joanne was an endless amount of coping worksheets for both of her classes. Joanne often participated in other school activities like helping to make pizzas for the after school pizza shop, monitoring runners in the Turkey Trot and also the dreaded bus duty.

Joanne was truly loved by her students. She gave them a sense of security and acceptance. Her kindness and patience was amazing, and she was tuned in to their special needs.

Joanne was always pleasant, friendly and easy to talk to anytime. She was a good listener and always had a story or two to share of her own. I looked forward to the few minutes every day before it was time to leave when we would kick back and chat about our lives, husbands, kids, good times, bad times, events, recipes, advice about this or that…then leave to walk to the cars. I remember our last walk out together on her last day at school after retiring. She was tearful, but knew it was time to go. You deserved a rest, dear friend. I missed Joanne then, and still do today.

Joanne,

I wish you happy days, peaceful days and days filled with sunshine. You have helped me through some very sad times, some very happy times and the very ordinary times. You've been supportive and caring on a daily basis. I know that no one can fill your shoes. You deserve only the best and I know that's what awaits you June 8th!

Love and best wishes.

Becky

KEEP ON Smiling And
don't ever stop

Smiling club
A group smiling

Sad club
A group not

Leader

Leader

Good by Mrs.
Sipka
We all will
miss you very
much

THIS WILL BE THE SECOND PART

THIS PORTION OF THIS BOOK IS ABOUT JOANNE AND HER STRUGGLES WITH THINGS THAT TOOK OVER AND CONTROLLED HER ACTIONS. THESE "THINGS" WERE SILENT AND SMALL IN STATUS BUT DANGEROUS. PEOPLE COULDN'T TELL JOANNE WAS STRUGGLING WITH ISSUES THAT WERE INVISIBLE. EVERYONE READING THIS SHOULD THINK IF THEY KNOW OF ANYONE THAT HAS THESE SYMPTOMS. ANXIETY, DEPRESSION, AND PANIC ATTACKS, PLEASE TAKE TIME TO UNDERSTAND THE DIFFICULTY IN HELPING THIS PERSON. WORDS LIKE "YOU WILL GET OVER IT" OR "LET IT GO!" MAY NOT BE THE ANSWER. I LEARNED SOMETHING FROM MY WIFE OF 63 YEARS, AND I FEEL BAD. I AM THE GUY WHO WANTS TO FIX EVERYTHING, AND I FAILED TO FIX JOANNE'S PROBLEMS. PEOPLE TELL ME NOT TO BLAME MYSELF, BUT I TAKE THAT RESPONSIBILITY FOR THOSE WORDS I REPEATED THE DAY I MARRIED JOANNE - "FOR BETTER OR WORSE, SICKNESS AND HEALTH, TO DEATH DO US PART. DON'T WAIT!

Joanne's Health

Joanne was aware of her health issues and took care of them promptly from the first day of our marriage. Her experience working for Doctor Rogers with children was valuable as our girls and grandkids grew. Friends would ask her about some issues, and I mentioned she should make sure they know she is not the Doctor. Her concern for health issues was a plus for our family.

I don't remember when she started to take drugs to help with her anxiety or when she started seeing a medical person for therapy. I probably said it would be OK or not seem concerned. It was like it would go away in time. But, because she was aware of her health, we felt she knew what to do.

She wrote a journal, and what she wrote indicates it was around the year 2000.

As she aged, she had diabetes but did not take insulin. Jo took her blood sugar test each morning and wrote the numbers to show the doctors. She would often make me prick her finger, apply the test strip, obtain the reading, and not tell the number because she was worried the figure would be high, which would upset her. I occasionally told her a lower number because she was so upset; I would say, "It's OK." I felt hopeless because I couldn't do anything. Her bouts of anxiety and depression lead to different doctors and therapists. These people introduced her to drugs that altered her mental state. I heard the words "Paxil" and "Adaval" daily. This new Joanne happened after she retired in 2001. I have included examples of her daily logs of her battles with these feelings. I want to help, but I am not sure what to do. The solutions are not like working on a math problem. When we moved in with her mother, she was busy and did not think about Joanne. She still had bouts, but Julia was her concern, not Joanne. I wanted to help and researched to help and not add to the problems. We bought a couple of programs with CDs to work through a series of presentations. A friend from church loaned us a series of CDs his wife used. I wanted to help but was careful to help and not hinder her improvement. Several pages of her daily handwritten notes indicate that she was fighting something.

Note – The description of Joanne's struggle with what I call the "THING" was obvious, and nothing I did worked. Picture a "thing" that can affect your thoughts, feelings, and actions. All family members wanted to help her, but this "thing" held on to her and would not let go. Having a new hip would allow Jo to enjoy simple things like walking in the house, visiting the store, visiting friends, and attending church. Maybe the "thing" was the combination of drugs taken to help her, but what combination? Was it something in her system? Was it passed from her family? Is it continued in our family?

Our family looked back and remembered when or if we caused a moment of discomfort that awakened the characteristic of panic or depression. Jo, at times, felt her daughters did not like her because they didn't call or visit. I wasn't enough. I can understand how a parent feels when the child is so busy they can't visit or call. Jo mentioned this in one of her journal entries.

She wrote these and fought this battle. She also was taking care of Julia as a caregiver. The struggles regarding anxiety, depression, and drugs to help these conditions were the enemy in her battle to have a normal life. She had a psychiatrist and psychologist and a family Doctor, Dr. William Reed, who prescribed Paxil and others. Adjusting the dosage to help by adding or subtracting was a guessing game.

Joanne's Daily Journal

<u>Joanne wrote the following in a journal for herself. She was told to write how she felt and not worry about how it sounded. I copied the same words to show the meaning of her thoughts and feelings because it may be hard to understand what she wrote. I have included copies of those five pages after the typed words</u>

#1 **<u>January 1st</u>**

Woke up at 6:00 toke Thyroid & ½ Zanx, went back to sleep, woke up hot arms at 8:00 & ate breakfast of cereal Stan made for me. Felt shaky & hot & cold – Stan went to church & I prayed on a card of different prayers. Stan came home & Norman and Mary came over & I tried to fight this panic because I didn't want them to see me like this. Finally, at 12:30, they left & Stan fixed me soup & I ate at 1:00 & took my blood sugar was 124 and my blood pressure & ½ zanax at 1:30. Now writing about it. Still fighting & I won't give in to this numbness feeling & now my eyes are closing, so it's hard to write, breathing labored, and maybe I need to fight more. I'm so tired now.

I was nauseated when Mary was here now it's past. Now I can't seem to keep my eyes open Take some deep breathes & keep writing. What else will help this attack. I'm trying to think of something funny like last night – The TV interrupted our count to midnight & Joey was hysterical. As a matter of fact, we all were screaming. What happened we were going to miss the count to 2010, We all started laughing & Melissa was crying because someone told her it was her fault & it wasn't. I felt sorry for little Melissa she didn't know what to say. It all passed so quickly. Now I'm trying to write – we left Carol's house & I was feeling good, not anxious like now. Got home at 12:30 or so & took my pills & fell asleep.

Now I feel tired, but I want to stay & I can't seem to keep my eyes open. It is 1:45 & I want so badly to close my eyes & go lay down maybe I will for just a few minutes. Just told Stan to come over to read to me What I wrote, but he was in the bathroom. Can't keep my eyes open at computer going to work on a puzzle if I can wait for it to load. I need to keep this panic out like the lady says. I can do it just try & things will get better all the time. Puzzle is taking forever to load, but I'll wait patiently because I am fighting this devil in my mind. Need to get over this on my own. I can do it. I can do it, I can do it. I am going to do it NOW, NOW. I don't know how to write it out any more. But here's the puzzle I'll make it work. Working a hard one, but I'll finish when Stan comes out. I did the puzzle now, want to write but going so slowly watching every letter to come out out of attack wanted to write clearly, but eyes are closing again. I'll try to keep my eyes and read what Lucinda says but I can't seem to read it now. I can do it! – I can do it! Just so tired. I want to close my eyes and sleep I'm going to lay down now & see if I can. It's 5:35 & I just sat down to write some more. My eyes are blurry now & I can't seem to see too well. If this is panic, It's the first time it has happened to me. I can't wait to eat. I'll go to bed early his evening I think because we were up late last night & threw me off schedule

January 1ˢᵗ

Woke up at 6:00 took thyroid + 1/2 gerot went back to sleep woke up hot arms at 8:00 + ate breakfast of cereal Stan made for me. Felt shaky + hot + cold- Stan went to church + I prayed on a card of different prayers. Stan came home + in a few mins. Norman + Mary came over + I tried to fight this panic because I didn't want them to see me like this. Finally at 12:30 they left + Stan fixed me soup + I ate at 1:00 + took my blood sugar was 124 and took my blood pressure + 1/2 gerot at 1:30. Now writing about it. Still fighting + I won't give in to this numbness feeling + now my eyes are closing so its hard to write breathing labored so maybe I need to fight more. I'm so tired now. I was nauseated when Mary was here now its past. now I can't seem to keep my eyes open. Take some deep breaths + keep writing. What else will help this attack. I'm trying to think of something funny like last night- The TV interrupted our count to midnight + Joey was hysterical As a matter of fact we we all screaming whats happening we are going to miss the

count to 2010. We all started laughing
& Melissa was crying, because
someone told her it was her fault & it
wasn't. I felt so sorry for little
Melissa she didn't know what to say.
It all passed so quickly. now I'm
trying to write – we left Carols' house
& I was feeling good not anxious like
now. Got home at 12:30 or so & took my R
& fell asleep. now I feel so tired but I
want to stay awake & I can't seem to
keep my eyes open. it is 1:45 & I want
so badly to close my eyes & go
lay down maybe I will for just a
few minutes. Just told Stan to come
over & read to me what I wrote but
he is bathroom. Can't keep my eyes open
at computer going try to work on a
puzzle if I can wait for it to load
I need to keep this going out like the lady
says. I can do it just try. things will
get better all the time. Puzzle is taking
forever to load but still want patiently
because I am fighting this devil.

in my mind. need to get over this
on my own. I can do it. I can do it
I can do it. I am going to do it now.
Now NOW NOOW. I don't how how to
write it out any more. but here's the
puzzle I'll make it word. Working a harder on
but I'll finish when Stan come rt. I did
the puzzle now want to write but going
so slowly watching every letter to come
out of attack wanting to write clearly but
eyes are closing again. I'll try to keep my
eyes open and read what Lucinda says but
I can't seem to read it now. I can do it
I can do it. Just so tired I want to close
my eyes and sleep I'm going to lay down
now & see if I can. Its 5:35 & I just
sat down to write some more. My eyes are
blurry now & I can't seem to see too well.
If this is panic Its the first time its
happened to me. Today Chris is bringing
us dinner so I can't wait to eat. I'll go
to bed early this evening I think because we
were up late last night & through me off
schedule.

Jan 1

147

#2 <u>Sunday, Sept 27</u>

We went to the cemetery & put roses on Dads Babies & Stan's mom and dads graves. We wanted to do this in memory – but I don't think Stan & I will ever get over our Angela's death. I only think of her as an angel & ask for her help getting me through all these rough days. She would have been 22 years old. That too long to mourn for her we need to do something else. I always said I'd love to donate something at Childrens Neo-Natal unit but now I can't take the stress. Dad was 100 years old on the 26th. He would be talking to me to try and get over this depression & live life its too short. I will keep trying because I don't want to live like this. Taking paxil all the time is OK but this other zanax is rough to get away from. I did cut it in half & now seem at a stand still maybe after all the tests are done I'll be able to cope. Barbara does help me realize it will happen.

#2 Sunday, Sept 27

3 <u>Monday, Sept 28</u>

Had a rough time this am. got up at 6:00 took thyroid laid in bed, and couldn't sleep so got up & took ½ zanax and ate breakfast at 8:30. Then was really nervous seem to need more zanax but I'll trying to wait. Stomach is quezy. Took paxil and ate lunch at 2:00 & more zanax. Now its 3:00 & I'm sleepy but can't sleep. Listened to tapes & they helped. One of my concerns is tomorrow if I can get up at 7:00 & go to school with Melissa I sure will try! One more week to wait for the thyroid test. I've had it 2x before & never a worry this time concerned but maybe for nothing. I pray! Its all in Gods hands. I do think I'm addicted to zanax and I'm trying to stay on lower doses. Think I'm not able to cope with lower doses So after these tests we will have to get some help. Also have a check-up with Dr. Reed sooner than Nov. & see whats up with my weight loss. I'm now 168. Like Stan says all my concerns are medical but when your stomach is upset what should you do. I know try to exercise. I promise to do more

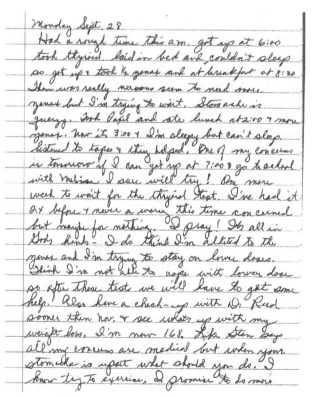

#3 Monday, Sept 28

#4 <u>Monday reference to an article in the newspaper (unknown)</u>

Fighting Panic attack all day because of newspaper. I feel like my kids had left me. I took a walk with Stan and came back & am trying to wash clothes. I am so upset about this article I didn't read it but saw the pics and it really made me mad. Trying to deep breathe & listen to tapes & now I will try to sing. I AM NOT A FAILURE.

Stan and I talked on the porch for a while and I need to learn how to cope. It is hard to always been put down by the 2 girls. And I miss the grandkids so much but they seem to have forgotten me.

#4 Monday reference to an article in the newspaper

150

#5 <u>MOOD INVENTORY – from a book that dealt with panic and anxiety</u>

It is best to read what she wrote. Note: I wrote fifteen statements from a MOOD INVENTORY, and she replied to the request. We talked about each reply.

The Mood Inventory has 15 items to answer. I wrote the questions, and Joanne wrote her replies.

1) *I worry and am anxious and depressed about what issues? (What I typed)*
   <u>HEALTH ISSUES WITHIN OUR FAMILY</u> (Jo's answers)

2) *The top three things I'm concerned about are?*
   <u>A) STAN'S HEALTH</u> *(these are Joanne's answers)*
   <u>B) MY HEALTH</u>
   <u>C) THE KIDS</u>

3) *The situations that triggered my worry, anxiety, and depression are:*
   <u>PROBLEMS IN FAMILY AND HEALTH CONCERNS</u>

4) *The worst possible things that could happen as a result of my 3 top concerns:*
   <u>Fear of Death</u>

5) *What would most likely happen with my top 3 concerns?*
   <u>Dr. with help Stan. I will need Dr. care too; The children have to get help from family.</u>

6) *What would be the best things that could happen as a result of my top 3 concerns?*
   <u>The Dr. would OK Stan's blood problem, Make my anxiety go away or get under control, and have Carol as her old self</u>

7) *I think about my top 3 concerns*
   <u>(   ) seldom (x) frequently (   ) all the time</u>

8) *Has my worry, anxiety, or depression helped to resolve or change the outcome of my situations*
   <u>(   ) yes (X) no (   ) uncertain</u>

9) *How valid are my perceptions of my problems?*
   <u>Some</u>

10) *What do I get out of all my worry, anxiety, and depression?*
<u>Nothing just more anxiety and depression</u>

11) *Will my worry, anxiety, and depression control the future of my problem?*
<u>   ( ) yes   (X) no   ( ) Uncertain</u>

12) *What types of things would be best to think about?*
<u>Enjoying my grandkids and thinking about my future home.</u>

13) *Am I willing to try to change my thinking and perception about my worries, anxiety, and depression.*
<u>Yes, I need some help, and where do I start</u>

14) *What advice would I give to someone in a similar situation?*
<u>Get some caring help to try to do what you want to do in life</u>

15) *Ten years from today, how will I look back on what I am facing?*
<u>I hope I can look back and realize I have to be the one to start to change. I can't control my family anymore and enjoy each one's success, whatever it is. I love them with all my heart and am sorry if I hurt them</u>

Mood Inventory

1) I worry and am anxious and depressed about ??
Health issues within our family.

2) The top 3 things I'm concerned about are?
   1) Stan's health
   2) My health
   3) the kids

3) The situations that trigger my worry, anxiety and depression are. Problems in family, health concerns,

4) The worst possible things that could happen as a result of my top 3 concerns are...? fear of death.

5) What will most likely happen with my top 3 concerns. Dr will help Stan. I will need phs care too. The children have to get help from family.

MOOD INVENTORY page 1 of 3

6) What would be the best things that could happen as a result of my top 3 concerns. The Dr would OK Stan's blood problem, make my anxiety go away or get under control. Have Carol as her old self.

7. I think about my top 3 concerns.
☐ seldom ☒ frequently ☐ all the time

8 Has my worry, anxiety, or depression helped to resolve or change the outcome of my situations?
☐ yes ☒ no ☐ uncertain

9) How valid are my perception of my problem? Some

10) What do I get out of all my worry, anxiety and depression? Nothing just more anxiety and depression.

11) Will my worry, anxiety and depression control the future of my problem
☐ yes ☒ no ☐ uncertain

MOOD INVENTORY page 2 of 3

12) What types of things would be better to think about? Enjoying my grand children Thinking about my future home.

13) Am I willing to try to change my thinking and perception about my worries, anxiety and depression? Yes I need some help and where do I start

14) What advice would I give to someone in a similar situation? Get some caring help to try to do what you want to do in life.

15) Ten years from today, how well I look bad on what I am facing? Hope I can look back and realize, I have to be the one to start to change. I can't control my family anymore & enjoy each ones successes whatever it is. I love them with all my heart and am sorry If I

MOOD INVENTORY page 3 of 3

Another example of what Joanne wrote – this has not been retyped and is difficult to read.

The two sheets are examples of what was used to help. There were two columns: a statement on the left and replies on the right.

2001

want to lay down   that will just not let me
                    see the sun.

never minded the snow
for 74 yrs   It is beautiful
cold outside   warm inside feel has
                  new warm sheets — I like them
                  so did Stan.

I don't know what to do   Looks good outside
feel so anxious its 2:40   The sun is out
This is not me I'm so sad
now Whats the matter I can't
see I'm crying
I felt like a failure   Stan helped me
                               talk this out.

This is the second sheet.

These are a few pages of what Joanne wrote about dealing with those issues. On the inside, Jo was not happy but delighted as she interacted with people. The involvement with personal matters was present when we moved in with Joanne's mom in 2002 but was less obvious.

Caregiver --- Mother's Death

Julia died on June 10, 2015, at home. She lived to the age of 103. Why so long? It was because of the care and love she received from Joanne. Jo had to stop thinking about being a nurse in 1955 because she didn't pass a chemistry course; the 13 years she spent caring for her mom as a full-time personal nurse were outstanding, even though she failed chemistry. The first few years were simple, just taking over the normal household chores – cooking, cleaning the house, washing clothes, and household bills.

Note- I am 86 and can imagine how Julia felt when we moved in. My three daughters worry about me now, as Joanne felt about her mom in 2002. Of course, me being 86 and Julia being 91, there is a 5-year difference, but I am like Julia, a little stubborn, and don't need help and feel I can continue.

In the last four years, we have included a lot of lifting and personal care. There was a cane, a walker, and a transport chair. When Julia had to be moved, Joanne was often the only one who could lift her mother. I became a helper because Jo could not help position her in the lounge or transport chair. We would position ourselves on either side, place an arm under her arm, lift her, and position ourselves to keep our balance. It was rough when we had to lift and turn her around to sit in the transport chair. We placed a guardrail around her bed, and she would kid us that we were locking her in bed. We would comment," That's because you go out after we go to bed!"

Julia was lucky to celebrate her 100th birthday with a party at St. Eugene's Hall. She enjoyed that day. She also had three more birthdays. Her brother, Joe, had Christmas parties for the entire family at a hall, allowing the large family to meet at least once a year. Diana would take her mom to mass at St. Eugene's several times during the warm months and lunch with friends after the mass until the last year and a half.

She was there when we made the Christmas cookies and nut rolls. Her role was as a supervisor rather than as the head baker. She had favorites, as did Joanne, so we had a nice variety of desserts. A week before Christmas, we made the caplets, and the house was full of activity. We would add the extra insert to our dining room table for more room. Julia would sit in a chair, make as many as she could, talk all the time, and entertain the family. The grandkids would ask her questions and make her feel important. She and the kids enjoyed the good laughs. When she was tired, she would move to her recliner and watch the antics of the "workers."

There was hospital care several times a week. Still, Joanne was the main person providing care. I would make breakfast and try different items. She liked the hot cereal with blueberries, walnuts, coffee cream, and milk. A treat she never turned down was ice cream.

Julia spent time in a recliner chair, which allowed her to change its position. She loved to crochet potholders, colorful washcloths, and slippers. Julia played solitaire with a deck of cards from 1967 and was worn down but didn't want a new deck. We knew she shuffled the cards to finish the game and was happy when she completed it. She read a lot and enjoyed the papers and magazines and her special television programs.

The visiting nurses came and stayed with her as her condition worsened. And the lady who lived 103 years said, "That's enough!" and died in her bed with family around her.

Joanne's Life after Julia's Death

Trouble began between the two daughters after the funeral. There were issues involving rings and items in a box that Dianne presented at a family gathering. I have never seen Joanne so upset with her sister. Joanne felt betrayed by her mother and thought her mom told her things about rings and jewelry for the girls and grandchildren. A box was presented; items were wrapped and handed out. But no ring that belonged to her dad.

I was next door talking to my neighbor when Joanne walked around the corner, yelling for me to come home because of what she had just experienced when she saw what Dianne had from her mother. We went into the house. She sat in a chair and was livid. Dianne and Ed went home. It took a long time for her to settle down that day and for weeks and months. We purchased the house. That happened in 2015, and Joanne wanted to make peace with her sister, and she did so around 2017.

88days ---- From July 18 to October 11

On July 18 Tuesday, Joanne had a successful hip replacement. She was looking forward to walking with no pain. She talked of long walks on the beaches at Hilton Head instead of the few feet due to the pain. Monday, the day before, she wanted to cancel the operation. Carol and I discovered her fear was taking her medicine; it made no sense because the hospital knew what she was taking and would continue the medication. She talked to the family doctor, and he made her relax and agreed to have the procedure.

We arrived on Tuesday. She went with the hospital staff, and we waited. She returns with a happy look on her face. Jo had numerous experiences where she would be nauseous after the medical procedure; this time, she smiled. Carol and I are pleased because of Joanne's attitude. In the late afternoon, she must stand up to start her therapy. The two ladies arrive; she tells them she doesn't want to do that now, maybe later, and they leave. They don't return. She doesn't eat much, and that's no big deal. She is moved to another room further down the hall, away from the nurse's station. NOTE – She should have been told to stand. It was my mistake not to persuade her to stand.

On Wednesday, Joanne had a happy look, and there was talk about the rehab location. We asked for Bath Creek, where Julia stayed; it was a good facility. Again, she doesn't want the ladies to help her stand and take a few steps; this is normal after this type of surgery. She has an excuse, and the ladies leave. I am a little upset with her not standing and walking, but I was told not to make her do that. (looking back, I should have exerted my request). She expressed fear and anxiety about standing.

After a few days, I started to keep a journal because it seemed like Joanne wasn't getting any better. I watched and asked questions and wondered what was happening to Joanne in a hospital with all this professional care. Do these people know what to do, or do they? Carol is a teacher and was off during the summer months, and took the overnight shift to watch Joanne. I arrived in the morning and stayed as long as I could. Someone was there 99% of the time in the three hospitals – Summa (City Hospital), Akron General Medical Center (AGMC), and Custom Critical Care.

Schedule of Joanne's Days in the Hospitals

On July 16, 2019, Joanne had the operation at Saint Thomas Hospital;

Friday, July 19, was moved to Summa (City Hospital) ICU. She said she had trouble breathing, and St. Thomas didn't have the units to help her.

On July 24, They tried to stand her up for the first time

On July 27, she sat up in a chair for the first time.

On July 29, she moved to a step-down five West;

On August 4, had fluid drained from the lung (first of six)

On August 10, Moved to the Bath Creek Nursing Facility

On August 13, she returned to City Hospital ICU because Bath Creek couldn't help her. Talk about a tube for food

On August 29, return to Bath Creek. (weekend of Labor Day)

On September 3, sent to AGMC ICU instead of City

On September 10, has heart catheterization

September 17, transferred to Custom Critical Care (We requested this facility for her first move but was denied.)

September 22, moved to ICU (We were told Joanne's condition was serious)

Was moved back to AGMC (date???)

She was in??? and said she had a taste for chicken noodle soup. A nurse brought her some, and she could not take any.

October 10, moved to Justin Rogers

October 11, died at 1:30 pm.

The above information describes the moves Joanne had for those 88 days. I didn't go into detail about medical procedures. The list would have been several pages more. The thought was to itemize what she experienced. The list indicated that her 88 days were a spiral down instead of a return to normal life with a successful hip operation.

The family contacted a lawyer and detailed her time with medical records from all the places for medical malpractice. We chose not to proceed.

Background Information

Joanne had periods of anxiety and depression, went to a psychiatrist for treatment, and was on various drugs. She was a person who wrote down times to take certain medicines and the quantity. There were bottles of pills with names I could not pronounce. She had spells where she would sit in a lounge chair and cry. I tried to help but didn't know what to say, fearing I would make her feel worse. I would kneel, place my head in her lap, and tell her I am still her little boy. I would say, "I love you." She would ask how much? I would straighten up and extend my arm straight out to the left and right as far as possible. "This much" would be my reply. As I mentioned before, occasionally, she would say she was sorry she couldn't provide me with a son. I would tell her that never bothered me, and she did a great job with our three daughters.

She wrote in a journal, and I would read it to understand better how she felt and maybe something I could do to help. These spells happened when we were living In her parents' house. Albert Braghieri died in 2001. Julia lived alone until 2002, when We moved in because Jo was worried about her mom. Julia was 91 years old when we moved. Joanne would stop almost every day on her way home to check on her mom; she did that when her dad lived. She retired in 2001, and her mom was 91 years old; this worried her. We asked Julia to move in with us, but she refused, thinking she was OK to live alone. Joanne spent many moments worrying about her mom and those simple things that could cause an accident. Julia had a pendant around her neck that would alert the paramedic if she fell or needed help.

We had a long, serious talk about this possible move. I was not in favor of it, and I was worried Joanne would move by herself and that I would be living in Tallmadge. There were hours of discussion. I mentioned we are both retired and deserve to do things we couldn't do because we both worked. Living there means we must wait for freedom to do "Our thing!". When we talked, I could only say that I could see her concern for her mom. She needed help, and we didn't. As I have said, Joanne was concerned about everyone, and here's her mom alive. Julia was stubborn and thought she could handle any problem. I said OK, and we moved in 2002. I owed something to Julia for what she and Albert did for us when we married. They let us live in their house, and that helped us financially. We will now postpone our free time. Julia lived to the age of 103 and died in 2015. We lived at 1925 Seattle St. for 12 years. We are 75 years of age. Time to do our thing!

Joanne had bouts of depression during this time. We had three daughters, all divorced, and were a concern for our grandkids. Jo's concern for each daughter, grandkids, and me was immense because she was like that. There were times we would sit next to each other and talk about the family and figure out if we could or not help. So much help was a money issue, but we were able to help. The comment was, "It's part of their inheritance."

One thing that bothered Joanne was Christine having trouble with her pregnancies. When Joanne was pregnant, the Doctor prescribed medicine to help her carry the baby. Years later, we found out that that drug caused trouble with births and did not help. She took this as a failure on her part as a mother. I talked to her about this many times when Chris had problems. It was, "If I didn't take that drug, it would be so different for Chris and Angela.

Julia Living on Seattle Street

During her first years here, Julia could walk with a walker and do things alone. We were informed of the house rules and had no problem. For example – <u>after taking a shower, wipe down the shower walls and the corners where the wall meets the tub.</u>

We went on vacations to Hilton Head Island, and I started playing baseball with the Roy Hobbs League. We enjoyed the week trip to Fort Meyers, Florida, in November.

We went from days to weeks to months and then years. Julia could move from room to room and had no problem getting in and out of her tilted-forward chair. You take each day and don't notice any sudden changes. She would often crochet potholders with colorful yarn and fill a basket to be given away. She was playing solitary with a deck of cards that was 50 years old. The cards' edges were worn down, and the numbers were hard to read. When given a new deck, she refused and wanted her old deck. She moved some cards but didn't call that cheating.

She can sit in her chair and needed help moving to her walker. She walks to the car to visit the Doctor. Diane and Ed take her to St. Eugene for Sunday mass and after to a restaurant for lunch. She gets her hair done every so often. We are taking care of the bills and the house inside and outside. She is in a transport chair and needs Joanne to lift her from the bed to the chair. I help Joanne move her from the chair to her lounge chair. It becomes the two of us needed to lift her, but Jo sometimes does it all by herself. I don't help when Julia has to go to the bathroom.

We get regular visits from medical staff and learn how and what to do. One man, Steve, was a physical therapist who made Julia exercise her legs. I wanted to do one exercise with Joanne in the hospital because I watched Steve do it with Julia. He would get Julia to stand up and hold her like they were dancing; the two were touching, making Julia feel safe. He would comment they are dancing. Julia was to move her feet a little like she was taking a step dancing. He would say they are doing "slow dancing." It worked for Julia but not for Joanne. We had a schedule board to show us when we had medical help. We had a ramp installed to help Julia in the transport chair.

Our lives changed to nearly 24 − 7 weeks of attention to Julia. Joanne worked many hours helping her mom. I could see her loving this caring; she had that feeling a nurse would have. Her early years of disappointment of not becoming a nurse disappeared. I wondered when or would we be by ourselves. We are in our 70s, and Julia looks like she could outlive us. I remember when Julia was in bed, and Joanne would sit in a soft chair in the living room. I would kneel in front of her, lay my head in her lap, and say, "I am still your little boy!" She would hold me and say, "Yes, I know you are." She would hug me, and I would back away and let her rest. She often asked if her girls would take Care of her. She was worried they would be too busy to help her. "They will, or we will," was my answer.

"They will, or we will" was true when Joanne was hospitalized for 88 days. The first three days at St. Thomas were no concern; she would be out of there in two days and after a few days in Rehab. Home with a good hip. No one stayed with her all night. After we all left Thursday night, She said she was having a hard time breathing and was transported to Summa (Akron City Hospital) and placed in the ICU with a respirator. We were notified and returned to City, wondering what happened and why she was moved to Summa. St Thomas does not have the ICU units that Joanne needed. She still has not been made to stand or walk. Rehab of the hip did not seem to be important.

She begins not to eat the regular diet for fear of choking. We would see full plates of food returned because she would not try. Baby food became her food because she didn't have to chew, and she would later refuse that. Finally, the hospital personnel came in and talked and showed her ways to chew and swallow crackers; she would do what was asked of her, and it looked like that person had corrected the eating problem. The next meal, her reluctance appeared again. I, at times, raised my voice and showed my impatience but settled down.

One day, I brought in a banana. Her plate had soft food and small-sized peaches. I asked if she would like some of my bananas. "Yes," she replied. I mashed up the fruit, fed her, and talked about things at home. For example, I asked her how to clean the kitchen cupboards with the oil she always uses. I was feeding her and talking. She would answer and tell me how she does that chore. I kept her busy talking about our house and those common cleaning tasks, and she ate all those items. I showed her the empty dishes, and she looked surprised. I told everyone what I did and didn't know how others helped feed her.

Joanne Had Someone With Her 24 Hours a Day at Summa, AGMC, and Custom Critical

Every day at City and Akron General Hospital and Custom Critical Care, someone was with her every hour. The three girls took turns staying all night. I could not stay, but I tried to arrive early in the morning. The grandkids also helped during the day. I was proud of the daughters and grandkids for keeping Joanne company for those 88 days. Diane, Joanne's sister, spent time with Joanne, too. Mrs. Sue Wells, our next-door neighbor, watched Joanne for a shift, which was a big help. Sue also wrote a tribute to Joanne. Our family appreciated her time, and I'm sure Joanne enjoyed Sue's music and company.

September 22, Sunday

Joanne is at Custom Critical Care on Market Street. The four of us were there and had a meeting with Dr. Patel. He starts the conversation with a statement that we should hear because of Joanne's condition. He mentioned Joanne's condition is critical, and her chances of recovery are not good. I kept thinking there would be some turnaround and those bad conditions would improve. I thought he was wrong! Dr. Patel said telling families this kind of news is the hardest thing to do, and he said he was sorry and left.

We sat there, were in shock, all crying. This can't be; Joanne will recover, you'll see. That was what we thought. The girls told me to go home, and I left. I was on the expressway and didn't want to go home. It's near one PM, and I remember the Kent Mud Hens (Roy Hobbs 65 and over team) might be practicing at Al Lease Field. That would be a good place for me to be. The guys are there; I sit in the car, watching the guys taking batting practice. I get out and stand behind the backstop, watching guys hit. Don Booth, the manager, comes by, and we talk briefly. I ask him If I can hit a few, and he says, "OK." So I am, concentrating on hitting a baseball with no thoughts of anything but the ball coming towards me. I missed a couple and then began to hit the ball. I thanked the guys and mentioned my wife was in the hospital but nothing about her condition.

Baseball came into play two weeks after October 11. John Elseg is a nephew and a catcher who plays on a Roy Hobbs team. He tells me he has me scheduled to pitch one inning in a practice game on a Sunday. I refused, but he told me the managers wanted to see me throw. So, I dressed and had several grandkids attend. It was great pitching from the mound with John catching. After the game, the guys from both teams gave me a signed ball and wished me good luck. My gloves are placed in a box for use later.

I wouldn't write anything about baseball because that's for me, but I want everyone to know how this affected me. The distraction lasted for one hour and went back to reality.

Close To The End

This book started when Joanne died on October 11, 2019. She was a beautiful person, and the world should know this. Jo was not a famous actress or politician, just a mother, wife, and caregiver to everyone. Her death was a surprise because I figured she would benefit from the operation and have time for herself and me. Our conversations were just the two of us. The kids and older family members had their lives ahead. She talked about seeing grandkids' weddings and great-grandkids. The hip repair would allow working in and outside the house and long walks on the beaches. There always seemed to be something we had to do for others, and then there would be time for us to enjoy each other. As the words appear on the paper, I imagine she looks over my shoulder, helping me with sentence structure and spelling. Our journey was happy, with few bumps in the road, just little ones.

I look at married couples now and imagine how they love each other and how the husband looks at his wife. Do they have strong feelings for each other? How did they meet? How long did they wait to get married? How long have they been married? I would love to hear how and when he proposed. Could their married life be a book? In today's paper, I saw the obituary of a lady who was mad at her husband because he died in his sleep next to her. I heard this at a bereavement session, and I told the group that I was sure he did not want to do that, but he had no choice.

I work or think about what has to be done. The journey around the house and the daily and normal chores require me to write information on the calendar.

Where Did She Go?

I was raised Catholic and went to St. Hedwigs Grade School till the eighth grade. The nuns talked of heaven, purgatory, and hell. They were places one would encounter years from now when one dies. They were just words. Those words became real on October 11, 2019, because part of me was going there. Heaven was Joanne's location. That was the first time I wanted to discover what Joanne was experiencing. Instead of me being so distressed, maybe I should be happy she is there.

After the funeral, Kevin Green, my sister's son-in-law, gave me a book about a man who had an out-of-body experience. If I had been given this book before this time, I would have placed it on a table and read it another time, but this time, I started reading the evening of the funeral. The writer was a brain surgeon and gave a lot of thought to writing what he experienced – he was pronounced dead and returned after several minutes. As I read more and more, I felt this was what Joanne was experiencing. It was what was best for Joanne and not me. Jo spent her life helping everyone; now she is with others she would know. Please, I was still crushed by her not being with me, but she is in a better place.

The author said he saw the face of someone he didn't recognize and didn't think anything about it until he was brought back from death. Days later, he saw a picture of a sister who had died, whom he never met (because he and his sisters were adopted), and that was his sister in heaven.

My daughter, Carol, visited a lady who told Carol Joanne was with a little boy and girl. I believe the two children were from our family, and Joanne has company forever. My job is to do what has to be done to get there to share her company. I hope I can give her another little kiss like the first one.

I have been around for 86 years and wish I was 23 again because my journey was great. It's all reminiscing now. I just told the doctor treating my foot problem to enjoy his two young children and wife. This is your best time having children and raising them to be adults to understand their duties in their family.

My Million Men Goal and The Reason For The Goal

I have a goal to reach 1,000,000 men with a request. Why? My wife died, and her absence is difficult for me. I wished I would have shown more attention just by a little kiss on the cheek or forehead. If I tell one husband this request, and he tells two others, and that continues, I can connect with a million or more husbands. To the husband, please give your wife an ever-so-gentle kiss on the cheek or forehead. If she asks, "What's that for?" or doesn't ask. Tell her, <u>"It's because you are here!"</u>

We take things for granted like the wife or husband will always be there. The surviving mate will be devastated by the void in their life. For me? I could never imagine the empty feeling I have now. I am getting the reputation of talking to men and asking them if they are married. If they are not married, I ask them if they know any married men and ask them to help me contact those million men. I am sure I have close to one hundred; just a few more to go.

Time To Close This Adventure

My family misses their mother and grandmother, but they are young and expected to live longer than me. They worry about me, and I appreciate that. I am stubborn and think I can keep going as I have for the past 86 years. The trick is to accept their help and maintain what I have been doing, only slower. I have to finish the projects – Jesus, Mary, and Joseph figurines, the "shut-the-box" games, and my little wood mantel clocks, fix a water leak under my sink, and anchor the gate alongside the garage. This resembles my bucket list items.

I spent a lot of time including details about Joanne and not me. Sentences were changed to emphasize Joanne and how she lived for those 63 years with me. I learned that writing is a form of grieving, and this has helped the last 23 months. I don't know how many more months I will grieve; most likely, it will never stop, but I will read what I have put on paper to remind me of those days' worth remembering.

Final Period

The final period is the punctuation mark that ends a sentence, a paragraph, and a story; it's a small dot that marks the end of this combination of words and thoughts representing Joanne Christine (Braghieri) Sipka. This is my attempt to tell the people who never met her what a wonderful person she was. She never wanted the limelight and enjoyed it when the daughters, grandkids, and I achieved some recognized achievement; she was our cheerleader. She was my partner sitting at the beach. When we returned to the unit, we would walk to the edge of the water and turn to each other, express our love for each other, and kiss—the perfect end to a day at the beach.

I have to add this story because it just happened. I went to the cemetery on October 11, the second anniversary of her death. I took a chair to sit in because I wanted to be there for an hour or more. I noticed a large maple tree about 200 feet away. There was a gentle breeze, which caused many leaves to fall. I saw one leaf moving towards me, just one, not many more because many had just fallen. That leaf came closer, closer, straight toward me until it stopped in front of me. I picked the leaf up, looked at it, and thought it was a message from Joanne. I thought it was saying, "Thank you for coming and remembering me. I can hear you; keep doing your job with our family. I'll try to help in my way, and remember I still love you. Are you still my little boy?" I nodded and said, "Yes!" and she smiled.

Holding hands on the beach

169

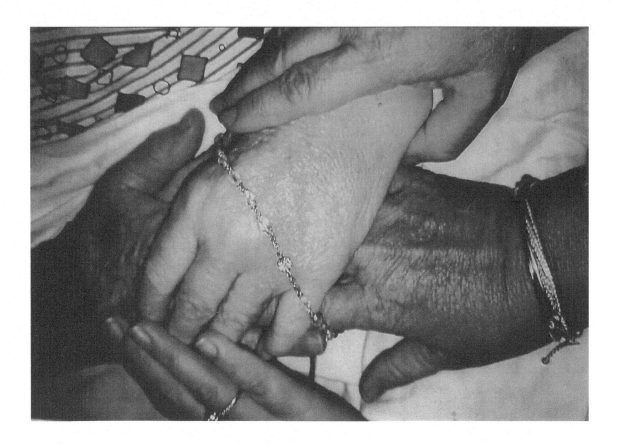

Christine, Cathleen, Carol, and I will never forget the last second we held her hand, and she went to Heaven. I have to get to heaven to be with her. I dream about seeing Joanne again and wonder if we could embrace, or could I give her a little kiss like that first one? And see that smile. She can show me around and probably tell me I am talking too much. I will be quiet and enjoy being with her forever (the final period).

Printed in the United States
by Baker & Taylor Publisher Services